Mastering
Human Resources

HSC Business Studies Topic 4

Graham Roll

This book is dedicated to the late Mike Lembach —
friend, colleague & mentor.

Five Senses Education Pty Ltd
2/195 Prospect Highway
Seven Hills 2147
New South Wales
Australia

Roll, Graham
Mastering Human Resources HSC Business Studies Topic 4
ISBN 978-1-74130-983-6

Contents

Rationale

This is a student topic book. Its purpose is to provide a concise, yet comprehensive coverage of the Human Resources topic in the HSC Course. Students are advised to seek other references and case studies in this topic because it is important to read as widely as possible in order to get the most from your study of the topic.

As far as possible, the material is presented in the same order as the Board of Studies syllabus.

This book includes a syllabus outline with Board of Studies outcomes together with the "learn to" aspects of the topic. Students are reminded that assessment task in Business Studies will always relate to syllabus topics and outcomes.

For case studies, students may find that useful information may be obtained by contacting the various chambers of commerce in addition to government departments and by using the internet which will give you up to date information in this area. Indeed, students who are aiming to maximise their performance in Business Studies should research these web sites and read newspaper articles for the most up to date facts and figures.

Topic 4

HUMAN RESOURCES

The focus of this topic is the contribution of human resource management to business performance.

Overview of content and outcomes

There are five major areas to be covered in this topic and they are as follows:
- The role of human resource management
- Key influences on human resource management
- Processes of human resource management
- Strategies in human resource management
- Effectiveness of human resource management.

4.1 The Role of Human Resource Management

- The strategic role of human resources
- Interdependence with other key business functions
- Outsourcing:
    - human resource functions
    - using contractors- domestic and global

4.2 Key Influences on Human Resource Management

- Stakeholders: employers, employees, employer associations, unions, government organisations, society
- Legal: the current legal framework
     - the employment contract- common law (rights and obligations of employers and employees), minimum employment standards, minimum wage rates, awards, enterprise agreements, other employment contracts
     - occupational health and safety and workers compensation
     - anti-discrimination and equal employment opportunity
- Economic influences
- Technological influences
- Social influences such as changing work patterns and living standards
- Ethics and corporate responsibility

4.3 Processes of Human Resource Management

- Acquisition
- Development
- Maintenance
- Separation

4.4 Strategies in Human Resource Management

- Leadership style
- Job design- general or specific tasks
- Recruitment, internal or external, general or specific skills
- Training and development, current or future skills
- Performance management- developmental or administrative
- Rewards- monetary and non-monetary, individual or group, performance pay
- Global- costs, skills, supply
- Workplace disputes:
     - resolution- negotiation, mediation, grievance procedures, involvement of courts and tribunals

4.5 Effectiveness of Human Resource Management

- Indicators:
     - corporate culture
     - benchmarking, key indicators
     - changes in staff turnover
     - absenteeism
     - accidents
     - levels of disputation
     - worker satisfaction

Outcomes

The 8 outcomes for this topic are to:

- evaluate management strategies in response to changes in internal and external influences
- discuss the social and ethical responsibilities of management
- analyse business functions and processes in large global businesses
- explain management strategies and their impact on business
- evaluate the effectiveness of management in the performance of business
- plan and conduct investigations into contemporary business practices
- organise and evaluate information for actual and hypothetical business situations
- communicate business information, issues and concepts in appropriate formats
- Also important to the understanding of your syllabus content is the section of the syllabus known as the "learn to" components of the topic.

Here you are being asked to examine contemporary business issues in order to be able to:

- discuss the influence of government on the process of determining employment contracts
- explain how businesses exhibit corporate social responsibility in the management of human resources
- analyse the causes of two workplace disputes and the strategies used to resolve them
- examine the advantages of a diverse, culturally competent workforce for a global business.

You are also being asked to investigate aspects of business using hypothetical situations and actual business case studies to:

- explain the interdependence between human resources and other key business functions
- compare the process of negotiating enterprise/collective agreements with the negotiation of individual contracts
- discuss the advantages and disadvantages of outsourcing in the global market
- evaluate the effectiveness of human resource management for one business and recommend appropriate alternative strategies.

4.1 The Role Of Human Resource Management

The strategic role of human resources

The strategic role of human resources involves the long term planning of staffing in a business. So far in this course we have looked at operations functions in a business, marketing functions and finance functions. No less important to the efficient running of a business is the role of human resources in a business.

If the business doesn't plan ahead to forecast it's staffing needs then it will be in the same position as a business that doesn't plan ahead with its needs regarding operations, marketing and finance.

Human Resource Management involves the use of qualified management staff in achieving the goals of the business, by ensuring that staff are productive, well-trained and satisfied in their jobs. The bottom line for any business is profits, however firms are coming increasingly under pressure both legally and morally to provide a safe and stimulating environment for their workforce.

Most Human Resource Managers have " staff authority" rather than "line authority". In other words they have the right to provide assistance to employees but not discipline them. They have the responsibility of running a smooth ship. They are responsible to top level "line management" to obtain the optimum performance from employees.

The Human Resource Manager is the line manager who directs all aspects of management relating to personnel within the firm. Their function is to ensure that their role as Human Resource Manager is in harmony with the goals of the firm that they work for. Indeed, Human Resource Managers now hold key personnel planning responsibilities in some of Australia's largest companies. Top managers are increasingly dependent on the contribution of their Human Resource Managers for organisational planning and strategy formulation.

Specifically the role of the Human Resource Manager is to:

- Identify broad needs within the firm relation to issues of employment (acquisition), induction and training, job satisfaction, job performance and rewards (motivation), employee benefits, health and safety issues as well as industrial issues (maintenance) and finally needs relation to retrenchment, retirement and dismissal (attrition).

Other functions which the Human Resource Manager can be linked to are:

■ Cost containment by maintaining an optimum sized workforce.

■ Improved customer relations through correct recruitment and selection and improved staff training and motivation

■ Social responsibility in areas such as fair dealing with employees, health and safety issues, equal opportunities and the employment and training of minority groups.

■ Once the Human Resource Manager has identified the broad needs of the firm he/she can set about:

■ Acquiring the correct staff. This is where the Human Resource Manager recruits and selects appropriate candidates to fill the vacancies that exist in the firm.

■ Developing personnel through induction, training and evaluation of that training

■ Motivating personnel by providing job satisfaction through such things as job enrichment programs, job rotation, performance bonuses and rewards- monetary and non-monetary. Here the Human Resource Manager needs to have a thorough knowledge of motivation theories.

■ Maintaining personnel by providing staff with, and making them aware of the various benefits and entitlements available to them. These include worker's compensation, superannuation, staff amenities, counselling and credit union facilities.

■ Providing health and safety programs and assist with accident investigations and their causes. The Human Resource Manager must have an excellent knowledge of the Occupational Health & Safety Legislation in their state.

■ Working and negotiating with union delegates on matters of dispute and working conditions under the "Fair Work Australia" Legislation and be able to advise senior management on ways in which matters can be handled so as to minimise disruption and loss of working time.

■ Terminating the service of employees. This is known as attrition and relates to the many ways in which a firm undergoes a reduction in staff. A reduction in staff can result from such things as retirement, redundancy, retrenchment, relocation and dismissal.

The interview is an important process in the acquisition of human resources.

Interdependence with other key business functions

As discussed earlier in this book, the study of this course should indicate to you that a business doesn't operate in little compartments of separate functions. Each of these functions are interdependent upon each other.

For example, the operations function requires a financial input or budget so that management can cost it's inputs into the business such as raw materials, facilities and human resources, cost its transformational processes such as technology requirements and monitoring costs and it's outputs such as warranties and customer service etc.

In other words inputs, transformational processes and outputs cost money and they have to be budgeted and accounted for. The finance section of the business must advise the operations manager about costing budgets and spending priorities.

In terms of the marketing of the good or service, as with operations above a marketing budget has to be made so that marketing costs don't blow out and that the right amount of money is spent marketing the product to the customer otherwise efficiency levels will fall.

Human resources have to be budgeted for and costed, especially since the cost of labour (human resources) is often one of the businesses largest expenses. Many businesses will pay top dollars to get the right personnel in key areas of the business because they will return high levels of profit to the business if they have the skills and personality. Even at lower levels within the business, staffing numbers can have an important bearing on the profitability of a business.

Outsourcing

Human resource functions

Outsourcing is a situation whereby a business contracts certain work "out" to professionals such as lawyers and accountants. This was (and still is) usually the preserve of smaller businesses which neither have the size nor financial capacity to employ any of these professionals on a full time basis.

Recently there has been a trend for businesses of all sizes to obtain staff through outsourced sources. Businesses have to do this because much of their work is specialised so they have to outsource in order to access the best talent available and also as a matter of economics. For example there are many companies contracting out their manufacturing processes to contractors all around the world who assemble the components and then sell them under a brand name. The Apple computer company doesn't assemble its own computers but instead contracts out its computer assembly functions and staffing requirements. Indeed this technique of contract manufacturing is common in the information technology and motor vehicle industries.

Businesses of all sizes and functions outsource. Many people think that only small businesses outsource because they are not big enough to have say a HR department, an IT department, a publications department, an accounting department, a marketing department and an operations department etc. This is clearly not the case; large businesses outsource as well, as the Apple example above demonstrates.

Many business contract work "out" to professionals such as lawyers.

Why do businesses outsource? And what are the advantages and disadvantages?

- Often the business owner doesn't possess the necessary skills to manage certain aspects of the business. For example they may not have any accounting skills, so this has to be outsourced.
- It is often cheaper to outsource certain functions to specific experts. If the business had to gear up to perform certain specialist tasks themselves, it could be quite expensive.
- Specialist firms are usually more efficient at carrying out certain tasks than a generalist.
- Outsourcing can provide flexibility of delivery rather than waiting for a division of the business to produce a certain component that they are not geared up to produce.

Therefore we can see that the advantages of outsourcing include bringing in specialist skills, cost factors, efficiency of production and flexibility of delivery.

On the other hand there are some disadvantages. Businesses may lose some control over the production process. They may find that they are not able to control delivery times or say industrial disputes in the supplier company. Quality control might also be an issue that can't be controlled and needs to be addressed. For example there have been complaints in recent times about the quality of service work being carried out on QANTAS air craft with some of the maintenance being carried out overseas where quality standards may not be as high and where it is more difficult to carry out maintenance checks.

With regard to advantages and disadvantages of outsourcing, like many things in Business Studies there is no right or wrong answer as such, only two ways of looking at the problem. Some firms may find it convenient to outsource and others prefer to carry out their operations in-house, depending on the nature of the business and circumstances. As a student you only need to be aware of the two positions and be able to comment on them.

Using contractors- domestic and global

Rather than employ full time staff, many businesses in Australia (domestic) use contract workers. A contract worker is someone who works for an employer for a period of time or on a periodic basis as required. For example, the tutoring business, Mona Vale Education Centre, uses tutors who are contractors. In this situation the tutor works for as long as they are required with a student or students. This arrangement can be terminated at any time by the tutoring business, the client or by the tutor themselves.

Regardless of this, when the student finishes their HSC exam or moves on to high school in the case of a primary student, the contract will come to an end and that employee will not be required to work with that student again. Once another student becomes available, then the tutor will begin again.

Tutors are outsourced as contractors in a tutoring business.

In many other businesses contractors are used, particularly in industry. For example, in the building industry, contractors are used to a very large extent. A builder would prefer to use a contractor to do the plumbing, electrical work and tiling etc rather than employ these trades people on a permanent basis because of the nature of the work. By this we mean that a builder doesn't always have constant or consistent work. There are often periods of time between jobs when there is no work and these trades people would have to be paid to do nothing. Alternatively, after a quiet period, the builder may have several jobs on the go and not have sufficient full time employees to satisfy the demand. Therefore the solution is to employ contractors who can be employed "on demand" when required.

Indeed, there are many industries that employ contractors rather than full time employees for the very reason outlined above. If work is spasmodic then contractors will be hired. If the business is small but needs occasional or regular specialised services then contractors will be hired.

Globally, many businesses use contract workers, particularly businesses which produce goods in an overseas country. It is usually cheaper to employ contract workers than have them on the full time/permanent pay roll. As in the domestic situation, the workers can be used as needed and the business doesn't necessarily have to set up large production facilities.

REVISION EXERCISES 4.1

1. Explain what is meant by "the strategic role of human resources".

   _____

   _____

   _____

   _____

2. Outline the role of the human resource manager.

   _____

   _____

   _____

   _____

   _____

   _____

3. Why do businesses outsource their hiring requirements?

   _____

   _____

   _____

   _____

   _____

   _____

   _____

4. Why do businesses use contractors both domestically and globally?

   _____

   _____

   _____

   _____

   _____

   _____

   _____

4.2 Key influences on human resource management

A stakeholder is any person who has an interest in a business in some way. They include:
- employers and employees
- employer associations and unions
- government organisations
- society.

Employers and employees

Employers or management is the group of people who own and manage a business. Employers goals are to produce goods and services, make a profit, expand and increase market share. Employers pay their employees in return for the work they do in the business.

Employees work in business for employers. Employee's goals are to earn good wages and achieve some level of satisfaction from their employment.

In a changing business environment, it is obvious that the way employers and employees get on with one another is essential to good employment relations. Areas of prime interest include pay, working conditions and hours of work, job description and job specifications.

As Australian business moves to compete on the global stage in the 21st century, both business and employees (often through their unions) have had to reassess their role in the process of employer/employee relations.

Already we have seen employers soften their attitude towards employees and unions in as much as they recognise their right to exist in a more positive and productive way. Employers recognise that employees at all levels are essential to the efficient running of any business and not merely cogs in a wheel.

Likewise unions have begun to recognise the right of the employer to make a good profit provided their members (employees) are not being exploited in the process. Indeed profitability is essential for the job security of their members.

Consequently, employers and employees have begun to enter into a dialogue which has led to an environment of much greater cooperation in recent decades. Part of the realisation by employers and employees that they "need each other" stems from simple common sense. Firstly, very little will be achieved for either party if conflict and confrontation prevails and secondly, the goals of each party are substantially the same---to increase production and productivity and therefore income.

Employer associations and unions

Employer associations advise employers of their rights and obligations with regard to their employees and provide representation at Industrial Relations Commission (IRC) hearings where necessary. Any employer, small, medium or large may have membership of their relevant employer association.

Some of the major employer associations in Australia include the Confederation of Australian Industry, The NSW Chamber of Manufactures, the Metal Trades Industry Association and the large Chambers of Commerce in each capital city. On a professional basis bodies such as the Australian Medical Association, the Law Society and the Master Builders Association look after the interests of members of those professions.

Unions represent employees in the workplace. The union movement began as craft or trade based organisations, but the modern union is based less in this way. Unions are now more broadly based rather than strictly craft or trade based.

There are many unions in Australia. The peak body being the Australian Council of Trade Unions (ACTU) which was established in 1927 to help coordinate the activities of all trade unions and bring them under one umbrella.

In recent years, unions (representing the employees) realised that to survive they must become more relevant to their membership by taking a more pragmatic approach to their employment relations strategies. Many unions amalgamated as part of an ACTU attempt to restructure the union movement and become more professional in their approach to the way they dealt with employers and their members. However, having said all this, there is still a long way to go in the industrial relations process before the system can be regarded as satisfactory. There are still many employers who are suspicious of unions and many unions which have not woken up to the realities of industrial relations in the 21st century.

Government organisations (state and federal)

Government plays a major role in the resolution of industrial issues in as much as it creates Industrial Relations Commissions (state and federal). It is in the best interests of government to ensure that there is a stable employment relations situation in their State or Commonwealth jurisdiction. An unstable employment relations situation can lead to political exile at the ballot box.

When agreement cannot be reached between employers and their representatives and employees and their representatives, the IRC through a tribunal, steps in to ensure the conciliation and arbitration process is undertaken as swiftly as possible in order to minimise disruption to business and the community.

The IRC and tribunals are not the only government parties involved in resolving industrial issues. The Anti-Discrimination Board hears cases of discrimination in the work place against any party accused of such on the grounds of race, religion, age, gender, marital status, sexual preference and physical or mental disability.

The Human Rights Commission hears cases of worker exploitation with matters such as employees being required to work very long hours or being maltreated in the work place.

The Equal Opportunity Tribunal has responsibility for ensuring that all Australians have equal opportunities in terms of employment, promotion and access to benefits in the work place.

Society

Society is a major stakeholder in the human resources/employment relations situation. The nature of human resource management is often dictated by the attitudes of society and the changing nature of society. In recent years things such as changing work patterns and population shifts.

Changing work patterns. Employment relations have changed greatly over recent years due to the changing nature of the workforce. Much of the workforce is casual, working at all hours of the day. Many people work from home and the workforce is more mobile than ever before. Rather than stay in the same job for life, many people will change careers several times in their working life. The workforce is prepared to move from state to state in order to obtain the job they want.

The workforce is prepared to move from state to state in order to obtain the job they want.

Population shifts

In recent decades Australia's population has changed greatly. Firstly, the nature of the population has changed from an ethnic point of view and many of these people are willing to move.

The Australian population has become increasingly mobile since 1970. By this we mean that the population is able to move geographically from place to place in order to chase work. Indeed geographical mobility has become a fact of life for many in the work force. Since 1990 the Federal government has moved to standardise qualifications in areas such as retail, hospitality, information technology and building and construction. This means that workers can move anywhere in Australia with their qualifications and have those qualifications recognised--because those qualifications are uniform right across Australia.

There has also been a trend for the workforce to drift from country areas to the cities in search of work as the rural sector continues its labour force decline. Other examples of social issues having an impact on the employment relations situation include maternity leave, child care, anti-discrimination, equal opportunity and equal pay, flexible working hours and home based work.

The current legal framework

Historically, industrial relations in Australia has been heavily regulated through government legislation. It is important here to briefly treat historically the changes that have taken place in the employment relations system over the years.

The government is involved in two broad ways through the legislature and the judiciary. As discussed above the government is a major stakeholder in the employment relations system.

Focus Point

An enterprise agreement is an agreement between an employer and an employee or employee group which covers wages and terms and conditions of work.

The legislature makes laws, relating to industrial relations such as the Commonwealth Conciliation and Arbitration Act of 1904 or the Industrial Relations Act of 1988 or the Industrial Relations Reform Act of 1993 and the Workplace Relations Act of 1996. Prior to 1988, most employment conditions were determined by Industrial Commissions which interpreted the laws made by the legislature (government of the day) and made decisions on the grounds of need for workers to receive pay rises or improved conditions and employers ability to pay.

Of most relevance to us is the later legislation. Prior to 1988 most working conditions were enshrined in Awards which determined the pay and working conditions of groups of workers within one grouping such as a trade such as plumbing, building etc.

The Industrial Relations Act of 1988 saw the beginning of enterprise bargaining in order to achieve an enterprise agreement. An enterprise agreement is an agreement between an employer and an employee or employee group which covers wages and terms and conditions of work. It saw the development of certified agreements which undermined the central role of National Wage Case Principles. A certified agreement is an agreement made between employers and employees regarding wages and conditions in a workplace which has been ratified and approved by an appropriate tribunal or commission. The terms and conditions of these enterprise agreements could now be ratified by the Industrial Relations Commission without any public interest test which applied previously, but subject to the proviso that workers were not disadvantaged. Certified Agreements could only be made between registered trade unions and employers. However, the take-up of enterprise bargaining and agreements was initially slow, with less than 10% of workers covered by enterprise agreements at the end of 1992.

The Australian Industrial Relations Commission (AIRC) was established by this Act. It is made up of a president and deputy president and industrial commissioners.

The commissioners do not have to have a legal background but must have substantial experience in industrial relations matters. To ensure balance in decision making, the commissioners are recruited from unions, employer associations and government.

The Industrial Relations Reform Act of 1993 was next. Under this Act, the then ALP government enabled the Industrial Relations Commission to process enterprise agreements negotiated between employers and non-unionised groups of workers. The major test for the Commission here was to ensure that such negotiations had been conducted in good faith.

Some employers and employer groups who dealt with strong unions saw a continued role for the Commission under the regime of enterprise bargaining. They would pursue a coordinated approach to such bargaining to ensure that unions did not pick off member companies one at a time. For other employer groups the attraction of enterprise bargaining was that it provided a means to by-pass industrial tribunals altogether. For the Federal Coalition and some employer groups enterprise bargaining held out the prospect of encouraging individual bargaining. Other than for a few legislated minimum terms and conditions of employment, the world of employment relations would be based on individual bargaining between workers and employers, with a limited or zero role for trade unions.

The Workplace Relations Act of 1996 was important to the recent development of industrial relations. The change of government in March 1996 brought with it a change of philosophy on how industrial relations in Australia should be organised. The Liberal/National Coalition envisaged that industrial relation was a matter to be determined at the workplace between the employer and employee with little or no third party intervention. In doing so they wanted to minimise constraints on the organisation's ability to have workplace specific conditions of work.

> ## Focus Point
>
> *A certified agreement is an agreement made between employers and employees regarding wages and conditions in a workplace which has been ratified and approved by an appropriate tribunal or commission.*

In 2006, the Howard Government introduced its Workplace Relations Amendment Act- Work Choices Legislation which greatly changed the structure of employment relations. It provided for:

- the establishment of a single national industrial relations system
- the establishment of an Australian Fair Pay Commission
- the creation of statutory minimum conditions of employment through an Australian Fair Pay and Conditions Standard
- greater award simplification process
- the establishment of an Award Review Taskforce
- a reduced role for the AIRC
- major changes to unfair dismissal laws.

This legislation was designed to further decentralise the workplace and give more control to employers when setting pay and work conditions.

Unions were concerned that workers would be subject to the whims of unscrupulous employers who would force unfavourable working conditions on employees and bid wages lower, particularly in situations where there was a surplus of workers. Unions believed that this would occur particularly with casual, part-time and shift workers. Unions were also fearful that their influence in the workplace would be diminished.

On the other hand the Howard government and employers believed the legislation would free up the labour market by allowing market forces to determine working conditions and pay rates.

However with the election of the Rudd Labour Government at the end of 2007, steps were taken to repeal the Work Choices legislation which took place in March 2008

In March 2009 the "Fair Work Australia" legislation was enacted which repealed many of the unfavourable aspects of Work choices. And on 1 July 2009 Fair Work Australia began operations as part of a new national workplace relations system underpinned by the Fair Work Act 2009.

The new system involves the Office of the Fair Work Ombudsman and Fair Work divisions of the Federal Court and Federal Magistrates Court which replaced that which operated under the Workplace Relations Act 1996.

The transition to the new system was implemented in stages via the development of two main bodies:

- Fair Work Australia- commenced 1 July 2009
- Office of the Fair Work Ombudsman- commenced 1 July 2009.

These bodies replaced:
- Australian Industrial Relations Commission (AIRC)
- Australian Industrial Registry
- The AIRC and the Registry ceased operations on 31 December 2009.
- Fair Work Australia assumed most of the functions of the AIRC and the Registry on 1 July 2009 and the remaining functions on 1 January 2010.

Features of the national industrial relations system include:
- a set of 10 minimum National Employment Standards (NES)
- modern awards that apply nationally for specific industries and occupations
- a national minimum wage
- enterprise bargaining, and
- protection from unfair dismissal.

The minimum standards relate to the following matters:
- maximum weekly hours
- requests for flexible working arrangement
- parental leave and related entitlements
- annual leave
- personal/carer's leave and compassionate leave
- community service leave
- long service leave
- public holidays
- notice of termination and redundancy pay
- Fair Work Information Statement.

The judiciary interprets and enforces the laws passed by government. This will happen when any individual, employer association or union challenges the law and asks the federal court or Fair Work Australia to interpret that law. For matters affecting industrial relations interpretations and disputes within one state, each state has its own Industrial Relations Commission (IRC).

Apart from interpreting the law, the role of Fair Work Australia and state Industrial Relations Commissions is to promote industrial peace and harmony and the prevention and settlement of industrial disputes. The state and federal industrial relations system is known as the dual industrial relations system with federal laws taking precedence over state laws.

> **Focus Point**
>
> *An employment contract is an agreement between an employer and employee/s that defines the rights and conditions for work*

The employment contract (common law rights)

Behind each agreement reached by employers and employees/unions is an employment contract. An employment contract is an agreement between an employer and employee/s that defines the rights and conditions for work and is usually enforceable at law.

The relationship between employer and employee is a complex one. It is based on common law which has evolved over many centuries in England and then inherited by Australia, because we follow the principles of English law. Since then this law has been affected by Federal and state Acts of Parliament.

As with any contract there are several conditions that are implied:

1. There is an offer and acceptance of work in a position for a given consideration (usually in the form of money, but may include such things as fringe benefits and superannuation).
2. The contract is a legal and binding one on the employer and employee in as much as work must be carried out in return for wages. Otherwise the employment can be terminated.

In any employment contract employers and employees both have rights and obligations:

1. Employers have a right to expect that their employees will carry out their duties in a competent and responsible manner
2. Employers have a right to dismiss an employee for breaches of the employment contract. They may summarily (immediately) dismiss an employee for behavior involving the safety or welfare of other employees. In other cases the employer must undertake remedial steps before the employment contract is terminated.
3. Employers have a duty of care and responsibility towards their employees i.e. they must provide a safe working environment for their employees to work in.
4. Employers must provide work for their employees if they are employed on a full time basis. When there is a shortage of work the employer must still pay the employee---they cannot be stood down for this reason alone.
5. Employers must pay their employees the correct rates of pay for all work carried out.
6. Employees have the responsibility to obey all reasonable orders and requests from the employer
7. Employees must act in the best interests of their employers by carrying out their duties in a competent and responsible manner
8. Minimum employment standards: These relate to the minimum conditions under which an employee can be employed and this relates to the section below in terms of wage rates, awards, enterprise agreements and other employment contracts.

Minimum wage rates

Employers are bound to pay a minimum wage rate or above to employees. Employers through their employer associations need to be aware of these rates. Fair Work Australia sets out minimum wage rates in such categories as:
- a national minimum wage
- casual loading
- special national minimum wage–for employees with disability which does not affect their productivity

- special national minimum wage- for employees with disability who are unable to perform the range of duties
- special national minimum wage–for junior employees
- special national minimum wage–for apprentices
- special national minimum wage–for trainees.

Awards

An award is an enforceable document containing minimum terms and conditions of employment in addition to any legislated minimum terms. In general, an award applies to employees in a particular industry or occupation and is used as the benchmark for assessing enterprise agreements before approval.

Fair Work Australia has responsibility for making and varying awards in the national workplace relations system. Modern awards are those awards created under the national workplace relations system which relate to specific industries or occupations.

Together with the National Employment Standards (a legislated set of minimum standards effective from 1 January 2010), they provide a fair and relevant minimum safety net of terms and conditions. The first modern awards were created as part of an extensive review conducted by Fair Work Australia's predecessor, the Australian Industrial Relations Commission. They came into effect on 1 January 2010

Enterprise agreements: An enterprise agreement is an agreement between an employer and an employee or employee group which covers wages and terms and conditions of work. Fair Work Australia can assist in the process of making such agreements, can deal with disputes arising under the terms of agreements and assess and approve agreements.

An enterprise agreement is made between one or more employers and:
- employees and (in the case of Greenfield agreements—see below) one or more relevant employee organisations (unions).

Awards cover a whole industry or occupation and only provide a safety net of minimum pay rates and employment conditions. Enterprise agreements can be tailored to meet the needs of particular enterprises.

What can an enterprise agreement include? Enterprise agreements can include a broad range of matters such as:
- rates of pay
- employment conditions e.g. hours of work, meal breaks, overtime
- consultative mechanisms
- dispute resolution procedures
- deductions from wages for any purpose authorised by an employee.

They cannot, however, include unlawful content (such as discriminatory or objectionable terms).

> **Focus Point**
>
> *An award is an enforceable document containing minimum terms and conditions of employment in addition to any legislated minimum terms*

Types of enterprise agreements

Approval processes for enterprise agreements vary depending on the type of agreement. There are three types:

- Single-enterprise agreements- involving a single employer or one or more employers (such as in a joint venture) cooperating in what is essentially a single enterprise (such employers are known as single interest employers).
- Multi-enterprise agreements- involving two or more employers that are not all single interest employers.
- Greenfields agreements- involving a genuinely new enterprise that one or more employers are establishing or propose to establish and who have not yet employed persons necessary for the normal conduct of the enterprise. Such agreements may be either a single-enterprise agreement or a multi-enterprise agreement.

Other employment contracts: As stated above, employers and employees have legal responsibilities to each other in terms of conditions of work. In this sense there are several other broad types of employment contract:

Part-time employees can be permanent except they work reduced hours. For example a part-time teacher may work two or three days a week. They receive holiday pay according to the amount of time they work and they receive holiday and sick pay.

Flexible employees work flexible hours according to need. The conditions here are similar to casual employees unless a permanent employment agreement is decided on.

Permanent employees receive benefits such as compulsory superannuation, holiday pay and sick leave. Usually at least one weeks notice must be given or pay in lieu of one weeks notice. However this notice depends on the nature of the employment contract. In some cases two weeks, a month or more may have to be given.

In each case the same fundamentals of the employment contract between employer and employee must hold in terms of general rights and responsibilities. Note that under Australian law all employees of all types must have access to compulsory superannuation.

Flexible work practices are patterns of work that allow organisations to operate more effectively. They can assist employees in effectively managing work and family responsibilities.

The main examples of flexible work practices are:

- flexible working hours
- part time work
- job sharing
- career break schemes
- working from home
- part year employment.

Flexible working hours allow employees to work an agreed number of hours spread over a set period of time. Some awards and enterprise agreements allow employees to accrue hours, take time off in lieu for overtime worked, and accumulate rostered days off as part of their flexible work arrangements. A personal carer's leave provision is now an entitlement for all NSW award covered employees allowing current and accrued sick leave to be used to care for sick and dependent relatives.

Part time work provides the opportunity to work fewer than the full time or ordinary hours. It provides employment opportunities for employees for whom full time work is not suitable, with the benefits of continuity of employment and pro-rata accrual payments.

Job sharing is a voluntary arrangement in which one full time permanent job is shared between two employees, each working part time on a permanent basis. For example, two primary school teachers sharing a class, working fixed days each week.

Career break schemes provide for longer periods of unpaid absence from work. Employers may allow an employee to take a career break for a fixed period of up to several years. Teachers employed by the state government can take a year off to further their study or for travel.

Home based work arrangements, such as telecommuting, enable employees to spend part or all of their working time at home, on a temporary or permanent basis. Contact with the employer can be maintained via telephone, email, fax or regular face-to-face meetings as required at the workplace.

Technology allows employees to work from home.

Part year employment allows the employee to take a number of weeks of unpaid leave in addition to standard holiday or long service leave. It is most useful for employees who wish to spread their annual leave entitlements to match school holidays. Part year employment can also relate to employees who work in seasonal industries and as such only work for part of the year. For example, people working fruit picking in the Riverina, prawning in the Gulf or driving a cane harvester in Queensland.

Family leave. Short-term leave to allow employees to meet family and community service responsibilities may be provided, for part of a day, a day or for a number of days. Examples of this could be to take care of urgent family responsibilities, being a member of the State Emergency Service (SES) or as a member of the Military Reserve. Employers and employees can negotiate additional entitlements through enterprise agreements. In 2010, the Federal Government brought in laws entitling families to take six months maternity/paternity leave on full pay.

Occupational health and safety and workers compensation (OH & S)

Another important legal influence is that of Occupational health and safety and workers compensation. Employers have a legal and moral obligation to look after the health and safety of workers under their care. OH&S is a legal requirement in the workplace.

Specifically, occupational health and safety is an area concerned with protecting the safety, health and welfare of people engaged in work or employment. The goal of all occupational health and safety programs is to foster a safe work environment. As a secondary effect, it may also protect co-workers, family members, employers, customers, suppliers, nearby communities, and other members of the public who are impacted by the workplace environment.

Under OH&S legislation businesses are obliged to provide:
- safe premises
- safe machinery and materials
- safe systems of work
- information, instruction, training and supervision
- a suitable working environment and facilities.

If they don't comply with these legal requirements they can be prosecuted and fined.

Workplace health and safety authorities in each state and territory and Safe Work Australia have responsibilities for enforcing the OH&S legislation. They provide information and advice on safety and health at work and education and training.

The New South Wales Occupational Health and Safety Act, 2000 aims to secure the health, safety and welfare of people at work. It lays down general requirements which must be met at places of work in New South Wales. The provisions of the Act cover every place of work in New South Wales. The Act covers self employed people as well as employees, employers, students, contractors and other visitors.

A paper developed and published by the University of Sydney in 2010 summarised the provisions and general duties of employers in terms of the Act as follows:

Employers must ensure the health, safety and welfare of their employees when at work. Things employers must do to ensure this include:

- ensuring that any premises controlled by the employer where the employees work (and the means of access to or exit from the premises) are safe and without risks to health.
- that any plant or substance provided for use by the employees at work is safe and without risks to health when properly used.
- ensuring that systems of work and the working environment of the employees are safe and without risks to health.
- providing such information, instruction, training and supervision as may be necessary to ensure the employees' health and safety at work.
- providing adequate facilities for the welfare of the employees at work.
- Employers must ensure that people (other than the employees of the employer) are not exposed to risks to their health or safety arising from the conduct of the employer's undertaking while they are at the employer's place of work.
- Controllers of work premises must ensure the premises are safe and that plant or susbtances used for work are safe and without risks to health when properly used.

Designers, manufacturers & suppliers of plant and substances for use at work:

- must ensure the plant or substance is safe and without risks to health when properly used
- must provide adequate information about the plant or susbtance to ensure its safe use
- design, manufacture or supply safe components and accessories for plant for use by people at work
- Anti-discrimination and equal employment opportunity
- As with OH&S above anti-discrimination and equal employment opportunity issues are also important legal issues.

Laws about discrimination are made at both the Commonwealth and the State and Territory levels. These laws include a range of grounds on which individuals may lodge a complaint including discrimination because of race, sex, disability and age.

Individuals can lodge complaints about discrimination, harassment and bullying based on these grounds with either the Commonwealth or State and Territory. The circumstances of the complaint will influence where it should be lodged. Individuals and businesses in all jurisdictions may be required to respond to these complaints.

Complaints about discrimination can be made in relation to a range of areas including employment, education, the provision of goods, services and facilities, accommodation, sport and the administration of either Commonwealth or State and Territory laws and services. From July 1 2009, most Australian workplaces were governed by a new system created by the Fair Work Act 2009.

Issues relating to anti-discrimination will be heard by the Fair Work Ombudsman. The Fair Work Ombudsman helps employees, employers, contractors and organisations to understand and comply with the new system. We provide advice and information, investigate workplace complaints and enforce Commonwealth workplace laws.

Complaints about workplace discrimination and harassment can also be made to the Australian Human Rights Commission or human rights and anti-discrimination bodies in each State and Territory. The Fair Work Ombudsman can help people who believe they are being discriminated against at work. They investigate allegations of workplace discrimination and can start legal proceedings against an employer for contravening Commonwealth workplace laws.

They do this to protect employees and prospective employees against workplace discrimination and any related adverse actions of an employer. The discriminatory adverse action provisions of the Fair Work Act 2009 are extremely broad in scope, and do not differentiate between direct or indirect, inadvertent or deliberate discrimination.

The Fair Work Ombudsman has a particular interest in investigating and addressing indirect and systemic workplace discrimination and discriminatory policies and practices. In other words covert or hidden forms of discrimination.

Unlawful workplace discrimination occurs when an employer takes adverse action against an employee or prospective employee because of a person's:

- race
- colour
- sex
- sexual preference
- age
- physical or mental disability
- marital status
- family or carer's responsibilities
- pregnancy
- religion
- political opinion
- national extraction
- social origin.

Other, more specific examples of discrimination can be:

- wrongfully dismissing an employee (e.g. unnecessary termination, retrenchment/redundancy, constructive dismissal, retirement)
- injuring an employee in their employment (e.g. limiting access to training/development; limiting promotion opportunities or limiting access to resources)
- altering the position of an employee to the employee's detriment (e.g. demotion, rostering– access to overtime/shifts, classification pay rate, employee benefits)
- discriminating between an employee and other employees of the employer (e.g. comparative workload/work complexity, harassment/ interpersonal conduct)
- refusing to employ a prospective employee or
- discriminating against a prospective employee on the terms and conditions of offer of employment.
- As described above, anti-discrimination legislation can come under Federal or State jurisdiction and many employers and employees would not be sure under which jurisdiction they fall. Generally, however if the employment situation falls under a Federal award then the Fair Work Australia Ombudsman would be the one involved. If the award is a state one then state legislation would apply.

Therefore, in terms of NSW The Anti-Discrimination Act 1977 (NSW) makes many types of discrimination against the law. The Anti-Discrimination Board of NSW is responsible for administering NSW discrimination law.

The Anti-Discrimination Board:
- deals with complaints of discrimination
- tries to prevent discrimination happening through education and training and
- reports to government if they think the law needs changing.
- Information about coverage of the Anti-Discrimination Act 1977 and about complaints procedure can be found on the website of the Anti-Discrimination Board. In many circumstances, the situation may also be covered by both Commonwealth and state discrimination law.

Equal Employment Opportunity (EEO) is a specific form of discrimination in the workplace. At one time EEO was a term relating specifically to the employment of women and their access to promotion within businesses. However it has now been broadened to include other areas as well.

Equal Employment Opportunity (EEO) is about ensuring that all employees have equal access to the opportunities that are available at work by:
- making sure that workplaces are free from all forms of unlawful discrimination and harassment, and
- providing programs to assist members of EEO groups to overcome past or present disadvantage (EEO strategies could include workplace rules, policies, practices and behaviours e.g. recruitment programs and access to training and career development).
- EEO groups are people affected by past or continuing disadvantage or discrimination in employment. As a result they may be more likely to be unemployed or working in lower paid jobs. These groups are:
  - women
  - Aboriginal people and Torres Strait Islanders
  - members of racial, ethnic, and ethno-religious minority groups
  - people with a disability.

Economic Influences

This relates to the state of the economy, particularly as it impacts on the viability of business and business expectations and investment. This could have been seen as an influence on the introduction of work place reform and in the move to more work place industrial relations with enterprise bargaining.

It is also known that unions are not as active during times of recession as they are during times of economic growth. Key economic variables having an impact on human resources and employment relations include:

- financial markets which when falling is likely to discourage employers from taking on new employees
- the level of general wage increases leading to fewer people being hired
- attitudes to downsizing and job cutting
- the capacity of the employer to pay
- levels of inflation which may or may not give the employer confidence to hire workers
- the levels of international competition which also may not give the employer confidence to hire workers
- levels of government funding which may or may not support employers taking on new workers such as apprentices. The government provides financial incentives for businesses to take on new apprentices.
- the productivity of labour, especially at times when technology is increasing and likely to replace labour with machines or computers.

Technological influences

The influence of technology has been one of the most discussed areas when it comes to human resources because the assumption is that technology will take away jobs and to an extent it has in some areas. However, for every job lost to technology, many more are created by the technology itself through the opportunities provided by that technology.

The reasons why some jobs are lost is that technology, specifically IT systems are often flexible, reprogrammable, and automatic or self-acting. They can record, process, communicate, and react to vast amounts of information entered by users, received from the environment, or stored internally. Good examples of IT specific to manufacturing and similar blue collar jobs include numerically controlled and computer numerically controlled machine tools, robots, computerised diagnostic and testing equipment, manufacturing process controls such as programmable logic controllers, automated material handling equipment, automated guided vehicles, factory local area networks (LANs), computer-aided design and manufacturing (CAD/CAM), material resource planning software to manage supplies and inventory, and flexible manufacturing systems that integrate many of these technologies into more fully automated systems.

Prominent information technology applications in office and service sector environments include common desktop applications such as word processors, spreadsheets, databases, e-mail clients, and Internet browsers; data entry and transactions processing systems (e.g. payroll, billing, bank transactions, and insurance claims) LAN's, CAD, automatic teller machines, bank networks for electronic funds transfer, electronic data interchange for automated ordering and payment between purchasers and suppliers, barcode scanners, and point-of-sale devices.

However as the Department of Defence Web site advertises, there are many replacement jobs available as can be seen below:

- Analyst careers analysing and reporting on intelligence affecting Australian Defence Force operations and Australian Government policy.
- Business management careers: broad range of administrative and management roles in a unique environment.
- Information security careers: providing help and advice to protect critical Australian information and information systems.
- Technical careers: highly specialised cryptology, programming, computer and network engineering challenges.
- Linguists: translating and interpreting diverse foreign material for a broad range of customers.
- Graduates: critical thinkers with problem-solving skills always wanted to join a great team.

These are just a sample of jobs in one sector. If one was to look through the employment sections of any city newspaper, they would find many jobs similar to those listed above which have taken the place of the more menial jobs of 20 years ago and this trend will continue.

Social influences

The approaches to human resources have changed greatly over recent years due to the changing nature of the workforce and changing living standards. Much of the workforce is casual, working at all hours of the day. Many people work from home and the workforce is more mobile than ever before.

Rather than stay in the same job for life, many people will change careers several times in their working life. The workforce is prepared to move from city to city and state to state in order to improve their living standards and to obtain the job they want.

The Australian population has become increasingly mobile in recent decades. By this we mean that the population is able to move geographically from place to place in order to chase work. Indeed geographical mobility has become a fact of life for many in the work force. Since the 1990s the Federal government has moved to standardise qualifications in areas such as retail, hospitality, information technology and building and construction. This means that workers can move anywhere in Australia with their qualifications and have those qualifications recognised because those qualifications are uniform right across Australia.

There has also been a trend for the workforce to drift from country areas to the cities in search of work as the rural sector continues its labour force decline. This is largely due to the decline in importance of the Australian rural sector which is in itself a reflection of increased living standards. Other areas to have impacted include maternity/paternity leave, child care, anti-discrimination legislation, equal opportunity and equal pay, flexible working hours and home based work.

All of these things are a reflection and to an extent, cause of our increased living standards which has necessitated/enabled workers to access maternity/paternity leave and child care facilities.

Ethics and corporate social responsibility

Ethics and corporate social responsibility is an important aspect of human resource issues from an ethical point of view.

Working conditions

Working conditions are very important to all employees. Everyone wants to work in a happy and productive environment. It is incumbent on all employers to provide this environment for all employees.

Some of the working conditions or benefits to which most workers are entitled to in Australia are as follows. (The first three are compulsory)

- **Workers Compensation-** This is a form of insurance paid by the employer to cover the costs of medical care and loss of income as a result of an accident at work. All firms in Australia are bound to cover their employees with this insurance.
- **Superannuation-** This is a form of deferred income. By providing a superannuation scheme it is allowing the employee to have an income upon retirement. There are two types of superannuation:

    1. **non-contributory** where the employer makes all the contributions
    2. **contributory** (often known as salary sacrifice) where the employer and employee both contribute to the fund. All firms must contribute to employees superannuation.
- Paid maternity/paternity leave (as discussed earlier)
- Staff amenities such as canteens and sports facilities.
- Counselling for staff experiencing difficulties in the workplace.
- Credit union facilities where possible.

Occupational Health & Safety

This was discussed in detail earlier, however it can't be overlooked in the context of ethics and corporate social responsibility. While it is a legal obligation for employers to adhere to OH&S legislation, many do not. However there are many benefits to the employer of complying with the legislation resulting in:

- more productivity due to fewer work days lost to absenteeism
- more efficiency from workers who are more involved with their jobs
- reduced medical and compensation rates due to fewer claims being made
- lower rates of turnover and absenteeism due in part to increased worker satisfaction and involvement
- greater flexibility and adaptability in the workplace as a result of increased participation rates
- greater selection ratios because of the increased attractiveness of the business as a place to work.

Some of the things that can caused accidents in the workplace include:

- too much noise
- interior air pollutants such as chemical fumes
- poor office design
- stress caused by demanding or inefficient supervisors, poor salary and lack of job opportunities
- safety issues such as inadequate footware or other protective clothing
- to comply with the legislation, prevent accidents and improve the health of employees many firms have set up programs to educate their employees with regard to OH&S issues in the workplace.

Some of these programs involve:

- safety instruction involving giving employees proper instructions on how to safely handle the equipment in their care
- general health programs designed to promote better health among employees. These may involve periodic physical examinations or a monitoring of an employee's health where they are in contact with dangerous chemicals, for example
- physical fitness programs have been developed by some companies to promote physical fitness among their employees. These programs involve such things as providing information on nutrition, exercise, weight control and the avoidance of tobacco, drugs and alcohol. They also involve the provision of physical fitness programs such as daily work-outs and other forms of exercise such as tennis or squash.
- health bonuses are sometimes provided by businesses to employees who follow a healthy life style and who say give up smoking.
- employee emotional assistance schemes can be offered to employees suffering an emotional crisis in their lives. Many firms provide councillors to assist employees going through a temporary emotional crisis.

- alcohol and drug abuse counselling is often provided to staff who are found to be abusing these substances. Indeed in the past employers and unions have jointly worked to assist workers to give up their habit
- stress management programs are important. Stress is a major inhibitor to productive work performance. If a person is suffering from job related stress then accidents can occur as a result of impaired judgment or at least job performance is reduced because of the fatigue and emotional trauma the employee is feeling. Stress management programs involve teaching the employee how to cope with work related stress. This is done through relaxation programs, learning how to separate work from home and physical fitness programs

The other areas of ethics and corporate social responsibility such as anti-discrimination and EEO legislation were also discussed in detail earlier so won't be repeated here except to say that these areas are also important in this context.

Finally there are numerous laws that businesses must comply with in the workplace in order to satisfy their ethical and corporate social responsibility and these include:

- Equal opportunity for Women in the Worklace Act widened to include other categories.
- Human Rights and Equal Opportunity Commission Act making it illegal to infringe on any persons human rights particularly in the areas of race gender, nationality, political affiliation, religious beliefs or trade union membership.
- Racial Discrimination Act prohibiting any race discrimination in the workplace.
- Sex Discrimination Act making it an offence to discriminate against any person in the workplace on the grounds of sex (male or female) marital status (married or single) or pregnancy.
- Workers Compensation Act provides an insurance structure for employees in the event of an accident occurring while they perform their duties.
- Disability Discrimination Act makes it illegal to discriminate against any worker suffering any form of disability (physical or psychological).
- Anti-Discrimination Act relates to any form of discrimination in the workplace on the grounds of race, sex, sexual preference, marital status, age as well as physical and mental disability. Any transgressions in this area can be referred to the relevant tribunal for a hearing and determination.

There are two other long standing Acts which all Australian workers take for granted and these are the Annual Holidays Act and the Long Service Leave Act. Both of these Acts guarantee that Australian workers are paid annual leave and long service leave after a qualifying period.

In each of these cases businesses have to comply with their ethical and corporate social responsibility, either for legal reasons or simply because it is the right thing to do.

REVISION EXERCISES 4.2

1. Define a stakeholder.

_____

_____

_____

_____

2. Complete the table below and outline the responsibilities of each

STAKEHOLDER	RESPONSIBILITIES
Employers	
Employees	
Employer associations	
Unions	
Government organisations	
Society	

3. Devise a time line showing the various industrial relations legislation that was enacted from before 1988 to 2010.

5. Outline the role of the judiciary in the industrial relations process.

_____

_____

_____

_____

REVISION EXERCISES 4.2   **Page 2**

6. Define an employment contract and list the essential elements of an employment contract.

_____

_____

_____

_____

7. Define awards and enterprise agreements and explain how they work.

_____

_____

_____

_____

8. Under the term "other employment contracts" there are:

    a. Casual employees

_____

_____

    b. Part-time employees

_____

_____

    c. Flexible employees

_____

_____

    d. Permanent employees

_____

_____

Outline the characteristics of each.

REVISION EXERCISES 4.2 Page 3

9. Outline how the Occupational health and safety and workers compensation laws affect workers.

_____

_____

_____

_____

_____

_____

_____

_____

_____

_____

_____

10. Outline how the Anti-discrimination and equal employment opportunity legislation affects workers.

_____

_____

_____

_____

_____

_____

_____

_____

_____

_____

_____

REVISION EXERCISES 4.2   Page 4

11. How do economic influences affect human resources?

_____

_____

_____

_____

12. Explain how technological influences have affected human resources in recent years and give examples of some of the new jobs that have been created by technology.

_____

_____

_____

_____

13. Explain how social influences, changing work patterns and living standards have affected human resources in recent years.

_____

_____

_____

_____

_____

_____

14. Ethics and corporate social responsibility are key influences in the human resources process. In one page explain the importance of working conditions and occupational health & safety to workers.

_____

_____

_____

_____

_____

_____

_____

4.3 The Processes of Human Resource Management

Acquisition

Acquisition refers to how employees are recruited for the firm. Factors to consider when acquiring staff include such things as the size of the firm and the type of employees needed, for what jobs and with what qualifications. Acquiring the correct staff is a critical issue in a business because staff are a very valuable resource. If the correct staff are not recruited, time and money is often wasted before new staff are hired and the old ones let go.

If a business has a Human Resources Manager who can see the "big picture" then recruitment policy will be aligned with the overall objectives of the business.

The interview is important in recruitment.

There are three broad stages in the recruiting process:
1. **Sources:** Where does a firm find a new employee? Through newspapers, Centrelink, within the business, recruitment agencies, head hunting and informal gatherings etc. To source lower level employees the company may simply work through Centrelink whereas a senior executive may be recruited through agencies, head hunting or informal gatherings.
2. **Costs:** Budgeting for the recruitment of staff will depend on the level of recruitment involved. The higher the level of appointment the larger the recruitment budget, and the wider the net will be cast. Senior executive recruiting may involve national advertising. At lower levels of recruitment, processes may only involve local sources and consequently at a lower cost.

3. Selection processes: Different types of jobs involve different selection processes. As with the example above the selection processes used to recruit at the lower level will be far less involved than those of a senior executive. Simple procedures may involve being interviewed for basic literacy, reliability and honesty whereas the senior executive may have to go through a large number of selection devices such as psychological tests, aptitude tests, interviews or even simulations.

Development

Once recruited, a business usually spends time and effort making the new employee a productive member of the team, making them better contributors to the goals of the organisation. This development process often includes induction and training. Workers will tend to be more productive if they have been inducted (introduced) into the firm in a systematic and meaningful way.

Induction

This is the systematic introduction of new employees to their jobs, co-workers and the organisation so that they are able to carry out their tasks in an efficient and meaningful way.

Researchers have found that formal induction can have significant cost savings for the firm by reducing the anxieties of new employees and by fostering positive attitudes and a sense of loyalty and commitment. Induction thus reduces the likelihood of new employees quitting before the bonding process is complete. Most labour turnover occurs in the first six months of employment.

Training improves the skill levels of employees.

Training

Training includes any procedure initiated by the firm to foster learning among its employees. The primary purpose of training is to improve the skill levels of employees and therefore help achieve the overall objectives of the firm. An effective training program will contribute to the employees job satisfaction and promotion prospects.

Education is very much linked to training but is broader in its scope and may relate to the upgrading of one's general education level, rather than to specific job training.

The Human Resource Manager is responsible for arranging a relevent training program. Naturally the manager would review the training needs and priorities in the firm. Those needs and priorities will vary according to the size and nature of the firm and the types of employees the firm has. This has to be coupled with the long and short-term strategic objectives of the firm.

Training methods can include:

- **Classroom training-** this is a formalised structure with a teacher or lecturer in attendance giving information. This can be carried out in the workplace or away from work at TAFE, University or a training college.
- **Simulation-** These are model activities used to imitate actual working situations. Simulation can take several forms:
  - **Simulators.** These are widely used by the airline industry and the armed forces to put personnel through training on precision equipment such as aircraft, tanks etc.
  - **Vestibule training.** A vestibule is an area set aside in a factory where workers can learn to operate machinery and other equipment in safety without actually being involved with producing something.
  - **case studies, role plays** and **structured games.** Role plays and structured games are often used to train executives and potential leaders. They are also useful as motivational tools.

On-the-job training

Training given on the business premises and can involve:
- **One-to-one instruction.** This can often involve having a mentor who looks after the employee's interests as well as their training.
- **Understudy** for a position in the firm.
- **Job rotation.** An employee learns to operate many different types of equipment. In doing so, the employee will discover how each part of the business operates.
- **Assignments.** An assignment is often a good way of 'forcing' an employee to learn new techniques and methods.
- **Secondment.** This is when an employee is transferred to another part of the business in order to learn that side of the operation. Sometimes secondment is with another firm for a period of time. Participants learn new skills which they bring back with them on their return.

Off-the-job training

This usually involves formal training courses. They are good for lengthy and involved training but sometimes lack the practical applications that an on-the-job training course might have. On the other hand, such training may enable the firm to acquire new skills and practices not previously available within the firm.

The use of technology

Through the use of computer aided instruction, the internet and DVD's employees are able to learn where no trained instructor is available or where locations are remote.

Improved technology in communications has been important in providing training in a cost-effective way. Wide area computer networks bring the trainee much closer to the trainer: the delivery of long-distance training programs is made easier.

Evaluation

Evaluation is essential to establish that the firm has an appropriate return on its investment in training. Has the employee learned new skills and are those new skills of benefit to the employee and the company? Training programs will be designed to enable a firm to pursue its mission: evaluation provides feedback to management to ensure training and business objectives are coherent. Human Resource managers evaluate training by:

- **Test results.** The results of formal examinations are widely used, particularly at the culmination of classroom based training. In some cases passing the exam results in a qualification and performance grading which may be used to rank employees in job selection.
- **Surveys and Questionnaires.** Reactions and impressions (of instructor and trainee) provide a useful guide on the value added by training. An instructor's assessment helps a manager or supervisor form an opinion about the value of an employees training experience.
- **Job performance.** How well is the employee performing his/her job? Are they any more competent and productive now? Comparing supervisor's reports before and after training will indicate if the training has added value.
- **Productivity and profit**. The effects of training on the overall performance of the firm is difficult to measure. Managers will form judgments about the contribution of training to productivity and efficiency. Such assessment, whilst subjective in nature, is a necessary part of planning and management.

Maintenance

Maintenance relates to the retention of human resources within the business. Employees stay because the business provides a range of conditions, including:

- a safe working environment
- job satisfaction
- good working conditions
- a satisfactory level of remuneration
- a career path
- job security
- fair and equitable industrial setting
- training and development opportunities
- social justice in the workplace
- providing a system of financial and non-financial rewards.

The business will establish administrative systems to manage and maintain its workforce. These include systems of personnel management that keep track of employees within the operation. Such programs are concerned with

- **Personnel records** such as changes of address, marital status, health and well-being, leave provisions and changes, return from leave data, etc.
- **Career Monitoring** Job data including training undertaken, transfers, promotion or demotion, salary changes, position changes.
- **Trends in Employment.** Technology may impact on the relevance of existing employees skill sets as the marketplace demands new products and practices. As a consequence, Human Resource managers will need to manage the introduction of new personnel practices to retrain and re-position the workforce.
- **Organisational Change** and its effect on employees. Employment policy will need to be managed to ensure the workforce copes with changes in the organisation.

Separation

Separation relates to how an employee leaves the organisation. Reduction of staff numbers occurs for a variety of reasons:

- **Retirement :** An employee voluntarily decides to stop working
- **Resignation:** The employee decides to leave
- **Redundancy:** Occurs when the firm is no longer able to provide work
- **Retrenchment:** The firm decides to lay off the employee
- **Relocation:** The job and /or the employee moves to another place
- **Dismissal:** Where a firm decides to terminate employment.

Voluntary separation occurs when an employee leaves of their own free will. **Involuntary separation** is where the firm decides to terminate the employment. When employees leave an organisation they are paid their accumulated entitlements such as long service leave and holiday pay. With redundancies and retrenchments there are usually additional payouts to compensate for loss of employment.

- **Retirement:** This normally occurs at age 65 for men and 60 for women, however many people are opting to retire at a younger age and take advantage of their relative youth and good health. To assist in their retirement plans many firms through the Human Resource Manager, provide programs that prepare retirees for life after work. These programs involve such things as investment planning and leisure planning.

- **Resignation or Staff turnover:** A staff member may leave their employment of their own accord. It could be to pursue other employment opportunities, move away from the area or dissatisfaction with their employment situation. In this case the employee is entitled to pro-rata holiday pay i.e. for the portion of the year they have worked. Any superannuation entitlement cannot be accessed until the normal retirement age.

- **Redundancy:** This occurs when a business can no longer sustain an employee because of economic or organisational circumstances. The decision to offer redundancy will usually include a 'golden handshake' (a cash payment)

An organisation may offer voluntary redundancy simply to reduce staff numbers. It may not expect every employee to leave but some employees may decide not to accept redundancy due to financial commitments. Those that leave will be paid out.

The firm pays compensation according to a set formula determined by government legislation. The formula relies on the number of years service and their salary on separation. The Human Resource Manager plays a major role in terms of human resource planning when it comes to the issue of redundancy.

■ **Retrenchment**: Retrenchment often relates to the laying off of an employee because of economic circumstances. A short-term downturn in the industry may trigger temporary retrenchments The employer may well be able to re-hire as the economy improves.

■ **Relocation:** Organisational change may prompt the relocation of the employees job to another place. Rather than offering the employee redundancy (especially if they are a valued employee) the firm may offer them relocation. If relocation is not accepted the company and the employee will usually negotiate a separation payment. To assist employees coping with the disturbance caused by relocation, it is quite common for the business to pay for removal costs. The employee may also be offered time off to relocate. Sometimes the employer will subsidise accommodation costs to help the employee and his family settle in.

■ **Dismissal:** If a company wishes to dismiss an employee they must be able to justify that dismissal on the grounds of gross misbehaviour, such as theft or physical abuse i.e. summary dismissal. If the employee is lazy or misbehaves in some minor way, there is a procedure that the employer must go through before the employee can be dismissed. On the occasion of the first offence the employee must be warned. On the second occasion they must be warned again and counselled about their behaviour. If this fails then the employee may have their employment terminated. However, all stages of the procedure must be documented to prevent charges of unfair dismissal. Again the Human Resource Manager plays a major advisory role.

REVISION EXERCISES 4.3

1. Define acquisition.

   _____

   _____

   _____

   _____

2. Outline the **five** broad stages in the acquisition process.

   _____

   _____

   _____

   _____

3. Define development and induction.

   _____

   _____

   _____

   _____

4. Define training and induction.

   _____

   _____

   _____

   _____

5. In **one** paragraph each describe classroom training, simulation, on-the-job training, one-to-one, off-the-job training and the use of technology as methods of training human resources.

   _____

   _____

   _____

   _____

   _____

   _____

REVISION EXERCISES 4.3   Page2

6. In **one** paragraph explain what maintenance of human resources involves.

    _____

    _____

    _____

    _____

7. Define the term separation of human resources.

    _____

    _____

    _____

    _____

8. Complete the following table:

TYPE OF SEPARATION	*V/I	EXPLANATION
Retirement		
Staff turnover		
Redundancy		
Retrenchment		
Relocation		
Dismissal		

*V = Voluntary/I = Involuntary

4.4 Strategies in Human Resource Management

Effective leadership is important for efficient running of a business.

Leadership style

Leadership style is the manner and approach of providing direction, implementing plans, and motivating people. Kurt Lewin in 1939 led a group of researchers to identify different styles of leadership.

This early study has been very influential and established three major leadership styles:
- Autocratic: Miltary establishments are run on autocratic lines
- Democratic: Decision making is shared by management and workers.
- Laissez -Faire: Individuals follow their own direction, remaining responsible for their actions.

Autocratic leadership style

This style is based on scientific analysis of work practices. It works well in a situation where staff are programmed to carry out simple repetitive tasks where there is single skilling and task specialisation and division of labour. Here leaders tell their employees what they want done and how they want it accomplished, without taking advice from others. Some of the appropriate conditions to use it is when the manager has all the information to solve a problem, they are short on time, and their employees are hopefully well motivated.

Where the business operates according to a strict formula, for example, a fast food franchise or a car assembly line, the leadership style is likely to be autocratic. Underpinning an autocratic management style is a highly planned set of instructions, based on the principle that there is only "one" best way of doing things. Time and motion studies are often used to refine work practices.

Democratic leadership style

The democratic leadership style can be closely linked to the behavioural theory of management in that it allows workers a high degree of participation in the decision making process as well as open communication channels between workers and management.

Typically the leader will encourage employee participation as decisions are made. The process invites input from employees, and the decisions are based on consensus. Often expertise and information is shared between management and employees, and clear directions only emerge following consultation. This leadership style allows employees to become part of the team and helps managers make sound decisions.

Laissez-faire leadership style

Laissez-faire is a French term literally translated as "let it be". In business and economics it relates to activity proceeding without intervention from above, or from outside the organisation. With this leadership style, the leader delegates the employees the authority to make decisions without necessarily consulting the manager, who is still ultimately responsible for the overall performance of the business

Employees make their own judgments, determine what needs to be done and how to do it. Management might set priorities but individuals control their own actions. To work effectively, the entire workforce will share the organisation's mission to ensure the business moves cohesively towards common goals.

Research organisations might typically be run along these lines.

Democratic leadership style allows employees to become part of the team and helps managers make sound decisions.

Adaptive leadership Styles

In some circumstances, a skilled manager may use all three styles, depending on what forces are involved between the followers, the manager, and the situation. Some examples include:

- Using an autocratic style on a new employee who is just learning the job. The leader is competent and a good coach. The employee is motivated to learn a new skill. The situation is a new environment for the employee.
- Using a democratic style with a team of workers who know their job. The leader knows the problem, but does not have all the information. The employees know their jobs and want to become part of the team.
- Using a 'laissez-faire' style with a worker who knows more about the job than you. The manager might not have much to contribute and the employee needs to take ownership of their job. The manager is released from supervision to be more productive elsewhere., doing other things.
- Using all three: Telling employees that a procedure is not working correctly and a new one must be established (autocratic). Asking for their ideas and input on creating a new procedure (democratic). Delegating tasks in order to implement the new procedure (laissez-faire).

Forces that influence the style to be used include:
- how much time is available.
- relationships based on respect and trust or distrust
- who has the information — management, employees, or both
- how well employees are trained
- internal conflicts
- stress levels
- type of task. Is it structured, unstructured, complicated, or simple?

Job design

Job design determines the way work is organised and performed. The process identifies:

■ the work to be done
■ how the job will be done
■ the skills, knowledge and abilities (capabilities) needed to do the job
■ how the job contributes to achieving organisational goals.

When a manager creates a job specification there are a number of principles to consider:

■ reducing job dissatisfaction by making the work interesting,
■ overcoming employee alienation arising from repetitive tasks
■ raising productivity levels by offering non-monetary rewards
■ providing job satisfaction from a sense of personal achievement
■ increasing challenge and responsibility.

Quality job design requires a clear understanding of the type and frequency of tasks that must be done now and in the future. Managers should consider why the tasks are needed to be done and how they relate to other roles in the organisation. In planning, it is useful to review the current arrangement of the tasks and if improvement is needed.

Good job design provides motivation and efficiency in the workplace. When specific tasks are broken down into component parts it is important to consider the well-being of the worker. This is especially so if the tasks they are doing are regarded as menial such as repetitive factory work.

Sometimes the human resource manager needs to create a job design checklist so that specific tasks are made more attractive for the employee. Below is an example of a checklist that could be used by management.

JOB DESIGN CHECKLIST

Variety of task.
 – Repetitive physical tasks use the same muscle groups.
 – Repetitive mental tasks may become boring.
 – Is there some variety or ability to choose what to do next?

Work/Rest Schedules
 – Static positions encourage fatigue.
 – Are there opportunities to change position?

Adjustment Period
 – Fast work pace promotes tiredness.
 – Is there opportunity to reduce muscle tension and stress?

Long work period(s)
 – Is there potential for fatigue?

Mental variety
 – Are there allowances for periods of adjustment.
 – Provide for varying pace of work for new/returning employees?

Training

Have employees had adequate training?

Job enlargement, job enrichment, job rotation, and job simplification are the various techniques used in job design. Good design increases the value of the position to the organisation, engages the worker and reduces individual and organisational risk. It leads to greater organisational effectiveness and efficiency and better results from employees. Key benefits include:

BUSINESS BENEFITS

- Increased productivity and efficiency
- Less need for close staff supervision, checking and control
- A skilled, flexible, responsive workforce trained in the right areas
- Targeted training to suit job design
- Improved talent management and succession planning
- Safer and healthier workplace
- Improved employee attraction, engagement and retention

EMPLOYEE BENEFITS

- Greater clarity of work role, purpose and accountability
- Shared understanding of work expectations with supervisor
- Increased job satisfaction and engagement
- Targeted training to meet staff needs
- Better career pathways due to job design
- Safer and healthier workplace
- Good team cohesion as roles, relationships and resources are clearly defined

Good job design provides motivation and efficiency in the workplace.

Recruitment

It is in the area of recruitment that the Human Resource Manager is seen to have the highest profile. This is because it is the Human Resource Manager who is doing the actual recruiting even though it may be senior management that sets the parameters of what is required. The Human Resource Manager will have acted in an advisory capacity in determining the requirements of the position and the type of person who would be best suited.

If the position is a very senior one, the General Manager or Board of Directors will make the final decision regarding the appointment of the successful applicant. The Human Resource Manager draws up the short list of candidates for the General Manager or Board of Directors for their final consideration.

In most instances within a firm it is the Human Resource Manager who analyses the job needs, sets the job description and job specifications and then goes about recruiting, selecting and placing the appropriate candidates.

The factors influencing the recruiting effort involve:
- identifying the need to fill a position
- defining the job
- preparing a job description
- specifying the requirements of the job
- establishing criteria concerning qualifications
- determining experience and skill levels
- personality testing.

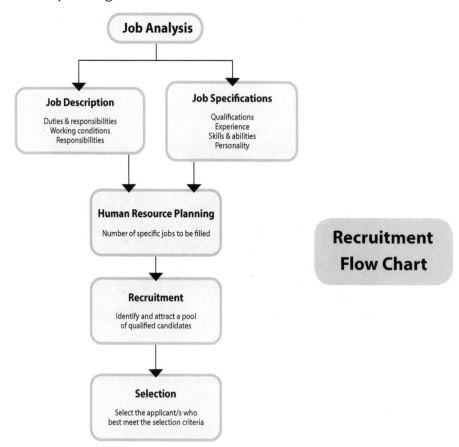

External Influences on Recruitment Policy

How does a firm attract staff? Internal sources are through promotion or transfer. Some companies in Australia have a policy of filling vacancies from within the organisation. Overseas companies use this method more than Australian companies.

External sources are from referrals, walk-ins, agencies, schools and trade unions. External recruitment is carried out via the medium of radio, television, newspapers, trade journals, internet and through companies merging or being taken over. Some employers recruit by **'head hunting'**. **T**he term head hunting refers to the practice of directly approaching a person who has the characteristics appropriate to a vacancy in the organisation. Sometimes, firms will conduct social gatherings to which they will invite the cream of the undergraduates or newly graduated professionals in a particular field, making offers of cadetships to the most suitable people on the basis of what they know of them and have been able to observe.

A great deal of controversy surrounds the notion of internal versus external recruitment. The advantages and disadvantages are outlined in the table below.

Internal recruitment

Advantages	Disadvantages
Improved morale of promoted employee	Inbreeding
Better assessment of abilities	Morale problems for those not promoted
Lower cost of recruitment	Political infighting for those not promoted
A motivator for good performance	Need for a strong management development
Have to hire only at entry level	

External recruitment

Advantages	Disadvantages
New blood and new perspectives	May not select the right candidate
Cheaper than training a new professional	May cause morale problems for those not selected
No group of political supporters in the business already	Longer adjustment and orientation time
May bring competitors secrets and new insights	May bring the attitude of 'This is the way we used to do it at my previous company'
Helps meet EEO needs	

The Selection procedure

A typical 'generic' selection process for filling a position is:

Selection Steps

1. Reception of applicant
2. Application form
3. Preliminary interview
4. Testing where necessary
5. Second interview
6. Background checks, references etc.
7. Third interview
8. Final selection by line managers
9. Medical examination
10. Placement on the job

At lower levels in the organisation the selection procedure may be less involved. More important appointments will involve additional processes.

Finally, when selecting employees internally or externally, the Human Resource Manager has to keep in mind changes in the demographic composition of the population, which can affect the type and availability of labour.

This in turn can have an impact on the firms Equal Employment Opportunity (EEO) and Affirmative Action policies. The increased number of women in the workforce is dependent on improved childcare facilities, the availability of part-time work, job security after an absence due to child rearing, maternity leave and special parental leave, including recently introduced paid parental leave provisions.

Legal provisions in government legislation and regulations increasingly impact on recruitment strategies.

Training and development Strategies

When determining training needs and priorities, decisions need to be made by the Human Resource Manager regarding:

- **Who will be trained**. It is important for the firm to identify the people who are capable of being trained and if those people will benefit from that training.

- **The aims and objectives of the training**. The aims and objectives of training staff in a particular area could be to fill gaps in the firm due to retirements and resignations. A need to increase the skills, productivity and efficiency of its workforce and to improve current and future skills of employees could also be relevant. Training in occupational health and safety procedures will usually be necessary.
  In this way current skills can be maintained and improved and future skills might be developed for the future needs of the firm.

- **The training subject matter**. The subject matter will be determined by the perception of current and future needs of the firm on an ongoing basis. Courses for senior executives, sales personnel, technicians or scientists and new employee may need to be restructured to take account of future trends. Future training needs may well require much more complex training strategies than previously adopted.

- **What training methods will be used**. Employees are beginning to determine their own training needs and priorities by identifying deficiencies in their own skill levels. Regardless of a firms's training needs and priorities, the Australian Government has recognised the need for training and development of employees in the nation's businesses through TAFE colleges, universities and on-the-job training.

- **What outcomes are expected**. As business strives to meet the demands of the global corporate world and pursue world's best practice in the 21st century, expectations of training program outcomes will be increased. Training delivery will become more sophisticated, especially using technology where possible. It is quite likely that key personnel will experience career path planning, and their training needs will be tailored to their future prospects.

- **How training is evaluated.** Evaluation will sometimes be subjective as measurement of results is often difficult. Some overall indicators of an effective training policy will be the financial performance of the business, and the extent to which this performance can be tied into HR policies.

Performance management

Performance management can focus on the performance of an organisation, a department, employee, or even the processes to build a product or service. An effective performance management approach would integrate and align organisational, departmental and individual planning and performance. It would also provide a means to recognise and reward good performance and to monitor underperforming staff.

Motivation is a key factor influencing performance. In some cases motivation may be the result of coercion by a strong supervisor; it may come as a result of peer pressure; or it may be self driven. If an employee enjoys job satisfaction they are likely to perform at a much higher level. However, the relationship between job satisfaction and performance is not clear cut.

Job Satisfaction

Employees will be satisfied in their jobs if they experience:
- mentally challenging work
- job enrichment, job rotation and Multi-skilling.

Poorly designed boring jobs promote boredom. Part of making a job more satisfying is the concept of **job enrichment**, making a job more meaningful and personally rewarding. **Job rotation**, the movement of workers between different tasks on order to develop their skills is form of job enrichment. **Multi-skilling** is also a form of job enrichment. It has the added advantage of increasing the flexibility of the workforce and increasing their productivity through reduced boredom. Other examples of job enrichment programs involve giving workers new and more complex tasks to do, increasing industrial democracy, adjusting work schedules and job sharing:
- work tasks within coping boundaries

Impossible tasks lead to job dissatisfaction:
- personal interest in the work itself.

If the mission of the business is held in high regard by the employees, they will be more likely to perform at a higher level:
- Rewards for performance.

Monetary and non-monetary rewards will boost performance. The recognition of an employee's contribution will increase motivation, productivity and performance. This is a result of someone obtaining satisfaction from a job well done.
- Work which is not too physically tiring.
- Pleasant working conditions.
- Opportunities for training, development and promotion.

> Strangely (according to research) job satisfaction doesn't necessarily lead to increased job performance, however the research does seem to indicate that good job performance can lead to increased job satisfaction.

Performance appraisals

Performance appraisals are a device used to review an employee's contribution to the organisation. In order to work efficiently and to assist in motivation, the employee needs to have regular feedback on the job that they are doing. The employer uses appraisals to measure the performance of their employees to see if objectives are being achieved, targets reached and if overall performance is improving.

What purpose does it serve? Apart from providing motivational feedback to the employee, it allows the employer to make adjustments to work practices and procedures, as well as monitor the work of employees and make further adjustments if necessary. For example, a wayward employee can be monitored and given the opportunity to improve, or an excellent employee can be rewarded and given positive feedback on their performance. In this respect it is one of the ways that the overall goals of the firm can be monitored. What are some performance appraisal methods that businesses can use?

> **Focus Point**
>
> *Performance management or appraisal is the process of assessing the performance of employees against actual results and expectations of the manager.*

- **Rating scale method**. This is the most common one and the one with which we are most familiar. It requires a supervisor to rate an employee on a performance scale. A series of standard questions are asked and the supervisor rates the employee by ticking boxes numbered 1-5, with 1 being the best and 5 being the worst. For example,

PUNCTUALITY
1. always
2. usually
3. sometimes
4. rarely
5. never.

- **Behaviourally Anchored Rating Scales** (BARS). This rating system consists of vertical scales with ratings 1-10 along the side and the employee is rated on the continuum.
- **Essay method**. Simply this is the writing of an essay or report on the performance of the employee. This allows the supervisor to point our unique features and characteristics about the employee that wouldn't come out using a scale or bars.
- **Management By Objectives (MBO)**. This method appraises employees by judging their performance against pre-determined objectives. Aims, objectives and targets are set out for the employee in harmony with the goals of the company. After the time has expired, the employee and employer review performance relative to the targets

they had set earlier. By agreement, the process is repeated for a further period.

■ **Checklist method**: This method simply involves a supervisor checking off a list of requirements for the satisfactory performance of the job. This is usually done by ticking boxes on the checklist.

■ **Work-standards method:** This method is usually used on the factory floor and is designed to determine what is a realistic output of work and what quality it should be.

■ **Ranking method:** This method requires each supervisor to arrange each employees in rank order from the best to the worst.

Performance appraisals should be discussed with employees to allow corrective action to be taken.

Rewards

Monetary and non-monetary rewards

When we think of rewards we tend to think of monetary rewards first but in the world of employment relations there are other rewards in addition to the financial ones.

Certainly, industrial harmony and job satisfaction is enhanced by financial remuneration. However financial rewards are not the only ones, or indeed the most important ones in the eyes of many employees.

As we saw above, money is not the most important thing in the workplace. Employees need something other than money to motivate them to do a good job. After all they are at work all day. If the work is boring or no recognition is ever given for a job well done, then the employee is not likely to be highly motivated. However, even though money is not the major motivator, it is still important.

At the lower end of the labour scale, most rewards tend to be group rewards and are in the form of money wages, superannuation and perhaps some company discounts on the products that the firm produces. However at the upper end of the scale compensation packages tend to be individual and are much more complicated and may involve some non-monetary rewards. In this case performance based pay is often a component of the salary package.

An example of a total compensation package of a typical Australian executive may look like the following:

Base pay (salary)	$110,000	54%
Employee benefits (superannuation)	$17,000	9%
Company car	$50,000	26%
Incentive bonus (performance pay)	$17,000	8%
Other	$6,000	3%

This can be shown graphically:

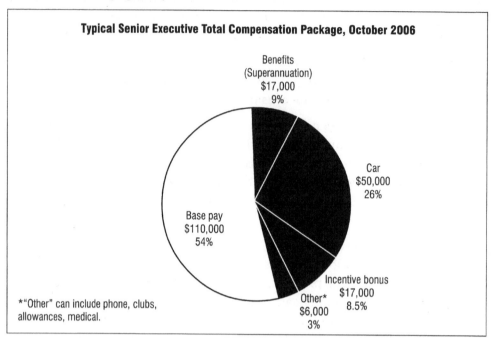

In broad terms, the components of a hypothetical total compensation package may look like this:

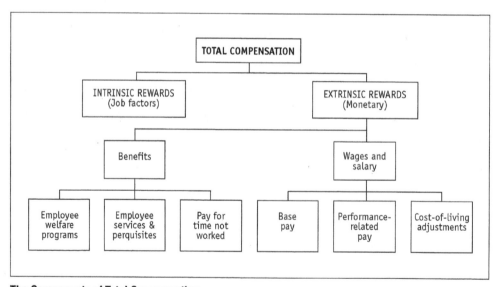

The Components of Total Compensation
Source: *Human Resource Management in Australia*, Schuler *et al*, p. 257

As well as wages and superannuation payments employees will often negotiate the payment of certain fringe benefits to their employees. These benefits are an indirect form of compensation that is often designed to minimise the tax that an employee has to pay. They are also an excellent example of a non wage reward designed to help promote industrial harmony.

At the lower levels of employment, fringe benefits are almost non-existent. However, at middle management level fringe benefits could include holidays, company cars, substantial discounts on the purchase of company goods, low interest loans and top up of superannuation. At the upper levels, fringe benefits may include things such as second cars for the spouse, payment of life insurance, club subscriptions, private school fees for children and telephone bills.

When the fringe benefits tax was introduced a number of years ago, many companies reviewed their fringe benefits programs. However, fringe benefits still remain an important part of many compensation packages, particularly at the top executive level.

Non-financial rewards include:

Training:

Recently, training and multi-skilling have become extremely important to the increased efficiency and international competitiveness of Australians industry. In addition any training that an employee undertakes makes them a more marketable person because of their greater skill level and therefore worth more money to own company as well as on the open market. Therefore training can be regarded as a non-wage reward.

Career paths:

This is another very important non-wage reward. In order to obtain the most from their employees management must provide a career path for them. Without one they feel they are in a dead end job, will have low morale and low productivity. However, if they think that they can work towards promotion with an increase in salary, status, responsibility and fringe benefits, then they are more likely to be more productive and therefore repay their employer many times over.

Equity:

Equity within a company is very important to the morale of employees. If some people are seen to be promoted over others because of their sex, religion, race, marital status etc then morale will fall and so to will productivity.

Job security:

This is also fundamental to the morale of the employee. Job security can promote good morale among employees.

Global

Costs, skills, supply

We live in a global environment and the globalisation of human resources has become a major factor influencing the recruitment of labour.

The international movement of labour has been growing since the 1960's, particularly in Europe where the movement of labour was encouraged by the regulations of the EU, which allowed and at times encouraged the movement of labour between countries belonging to the EU.

About 2.5% of the world's population live outside their country of birth. As communications improve, in particular the World Wide Web it allows people to access and apply for jobs all over the world. Large corporations actively aim to attract scarce labour in this way. The communications revolution allows for the movement of 'intelligence' i.e. workers who have particular skills or qualifications are attracted to move from one country to another in order to improve their salaries.

Scarcity of labour leads to increased costs of hiring that labour. In many cases businesses must look overseas to recruit labour. In many cases when the supply of skilled workers doesn't exist in Australia then businesses must look overseas for that labour.

Workplace disputes

An important aspect of human resource management strategies is that of resolving workplace disputes. What are workplace disputes? There is no 'textbook' definition of a workplace dispute but suffice it to say that it is a situation in which employers and employees are in dispute with one another over some aspect of the employment contract. When a disagreement occurs and talks between management and unions/employees breaks down then a conflict or dispute exists.

The Australian Bureau of Statistics categorises the causes of industrial disputes into eight broad groups. They are:

Wage demands

The most obvious cause and most often publicised. However wage disputes have fallen from 30% to about 8% in recent years.

Hours of work

This is only a small component of industrial conflict, being less than 1% of all disputes. However it covers such things as overtime, rosters and changes in the length of the working day or week.

Leave, pensions & compensation

Around 6% of industrial disputes fall into this category and relate often to items such as redundancy payments for retrenched workers, the calculation of entitlement to holiday pay and long service leave as well as worker's compensation provisions.

Management policy

Disputation in this area has risen from 35% of all disputes in 1980 to 60% in recent years. A good example of this has been the various disputes at QANTAS between management and baggage handlers over the weight of bags that workers are expected to lift.

Working conditions

This area involves such things as the availability of protective clothing and equipment, the provision of first aid facilities, the availability and quality of amenities such as change rooms, toilet facilities, the physical conditions associated with the job and the availability and quality of work equipment.

Trade unionism

This area includes the employment of non-unionists, demarcation disputes, inter-union disputes and sympathy stoppages.

Political Goals

This covers disputes not directly related to employment including industrial action in pursuit of political objectives. A good example of this would be a general strike by unions to protest against some form of government decisions.

Social Issues

As with the political goals above, social issues such as human rights issues, ecological issues at home in Australia or overseas might precipitate industrial conflict. Social issues that may cause industrial conflict could be the improper treatment of employees on racial, sex, marital, age or disability grounds.

In order to have a full understanding of how employment relations issues are resolved, it is important to revisit who the stakeholders are. They are:

1. Employers who are in dispute with employees. In small firms negotiations will usually be carried out with the owner or managing director in an informal way. If the dispute is a large one, the employer association will again supply an industrial advocate to assist.
2. Employer associations advise employers of their rights and obligations with regard to their employees and provide representation at IRC hearings if necessary.
3. Employees/unions who have a grievance with the employer. In small businesses employees may or may not be members of the union.

In many cases they refuse to join because of long standing good relationships with their employers. However if a dispute does arise they must negotiate on their own behalf with the owner. If the employees are members of the union, then a union representative will visit the premises and negotiate on their behalf.

4. Government plays a major role in the resolution of industrial issues in as much as it creates Industrial Relations Commissions (state and federal). When agreement cannot be reached between employers and their representatives and employees and their representatives, the IRC through a tribunal steps in to ensure the conciliation and arbitration process is undertaken as swiftly as possible in order to minimise disruption to business and the community.

Some of the boards, commissions and tribunals set up by the government include:

- The Anti-Discrimination Board hears cases of discrimination in the work place.
- The Human Rights Commission hears cases of worker exploitation with regard to matters such as employees being required to work very long hours or being mal treated in the work place.
- The Equal Opportunity Tribunal has responsibility for ensuring that all Australians have equal opportunities in terms of employment, promotion and access to benefits in the work place.

Dispute resolution process

Having considered the stakeholders involved in resolving industrial issues, we will now turn our attention to the processes by which industrial issues are resolved. In order for the processes to come into play there has to be a dispute. This may seem obvious, but there are procedures that both parties in the dispute must follow before the processes can begin.

These procedures will follow along the following lines:

- Firstly, a log of claims is served on the employer by the union- usually more than they want or hope to achieve. This is known as an ambit claim. Unions do this because they know that they can bargain downwards from this position i.e. it gives them bargaining space.
- Employers then prepare and present a counter log of claims outlining where they stand with regard to the unions claims. Because the log of claims presented by the union is an ambit one, the employers log will fall far short of the union demands. The difference between the two sets the limits of the dispute. Any decision reached will have to fall within those limits. It is then that negotiations begin in earnest.

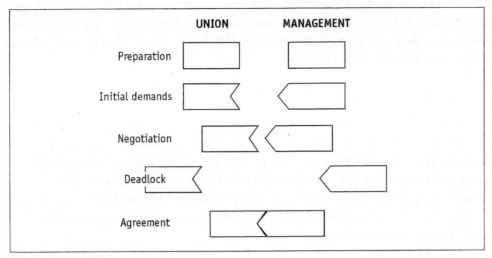

Stages of Negotiation
Source: *Human Resource Management*, Schuler *et al*, p.375

The diagram above shows the initial preparation of a log of claims by both parties, the initial (ambit) claim, the negotiation setting the limits of the dispute, the deadlock (now involving conciliation and arbitration) and finally the agreement.

Grievance procedures

These procedures have been included in awards for many years but have largely been ignored. In recent years the IRC has encouraged parties to use these procedures in the first instance in the hope of avoiding more protracted disputes. Grievance procedures work like this.

The first step is for the grievance to be taken to an immediate supervisor who is obliged to reply as soon as possible or issue a progress report if there is likely to be any delay. If the matter is not resolved it must be taken to the next level of supervision where the parties again attempt to reach agreement. If the matter is still not resolved it must go to senior management, the industrial relations manager or human resources manager. Full time union officials are also involved at this stage. Failing resolution at this stage the matter will be referred to the appropriate industrial tribunal.

Conciliation and Arbitration

Once the steps above have been taken, either party to the dispute can inform the industrial registrar and request a formal conference. In this case a commissioner will order a compulsory conference of the two parties either alone or in the presence of a commissioner. If the commissioner is present he/she will mediate in the dispute. If this fails then the two parties must enter the stage of arbitration. Here a commissioner listens to the arguments of both sides presented to him/her by the advocates representing each party.

The decision brought down by the commissioner is in the form of an award or order and is legally binding on both parties. Either party may appeal the decision if they disagree with the commissioners ruling. This appeal is heard by the Full Bench of the IRC.

Negotiation

Negotiation is the process of setting the limits of a dispute and discussing where each party stands. This involves compromise and offer over the discussion table. Sometimes a dispute can be settled quickly using this process, but at other times the negotiation process fails because the conflicting parties cannot agree on a negotiated settlement. This occurs because one or both parties are not prepared to move (or not move far enough) from their stated position.

Mediation

Mediation occurs when a third party who is mutually acceptable and neutral, sits down with both parties and hears the dispute. The idea of using a mediator is to try to diffuse the issue and take the heat out of the dispute. Both parties are happy because the mediator has no bias in the situation.

Common law action

Sometimes one party in an industrial conflict has to resort to common law action to resolve a dispute. Common law is based on the decision of a judge to solve a dispute.

Collective bargaining

This is a method of negotiation between employer and employee. Usually the employer is represented by their employer association, and the employees by their union. This system simply amounts to the two parties and their representatives sitting down and thrashing out their differences.

Enterprise bargaining

This is similar to collective bargaining except that the purpose of enterprise bargaining is to try to establish pay and conditions of work rather than to resolve an industrial dispute (that is not to say there is no disputation in the process).

Business/division closure

Occasionally, a conflict may only be resolved by closing down all or part of a business. This is not an often occurrence but still may occur if a conflict is not resolved.

REVISION EXERCISES 4.4

1. Explain what is meant by the term 'leadership style'.

_____

_____

_____

_____

_____

_____

_____

_____

_____

2. Complete the following table:

Leadership Style	Characteristics
Authoritarian/autocratic	
Participative/democratic	
Delegative/free reign	

3. Define 'job design' and outline the processes that occur.

_____

_____

_____

_____

_____

_____

_____

_____

_____

_____

_____

4. Complete the following:

Sources of Job Applicants

Internal

Advantages   Disadvantages

_____   _____

_____   _____

External

Advantages   Disadvantages

_____   _____

_____   _____

5. Define the 'Training and development' and 'Induction'.

_____

_____

_____

6. When determining training needs and priorities, decisions need to be made by the Human Resource Manager. List the six training needs and priorities.

_____

_____

_____

_____

_____

_____

_____

_____

_____

_____

_____

_____

_____

7. In **half a page,** summarise the various training methods used by businesses.

_____

_____

_____

_____

_____

_____

_____

_____

_____

_____

_____

_____

_____

_____

_____

8. Define and explain the concept of performance management.

_____

_____

_____

_____

_____

_____

_____

_____

_____

_____

_____

_____

_____

10. Explain the difference between monetary and non-monetary rewards and give three examples of each.

_____

_____

_____

_____

_____

_____

_____

11. List the **eight** the causes of industrial disputes.

_____

_____

_____

_____

_____

_____

_____

13. List the **four** key stakeholders in the employment relations process and outline what their interest in the process is.

_____

_____

_____

_____

_____

_____

15. Summarise the section on 'dispute resolution processes'.

_____

_____

_____

_____

_____

_____

_____

4.5 Effectiveness of human resource management

If the workforce in a business is to be productive and help the firm achieve its' overall objectives, management must measure the effectiveness of that workforce. For a workforce to be regarded as effective, staff will be well trained, focused and satisfied at work. There are a number of indicators that effect human resource management and ensure practices are in place.

Corporate Culture

A good corporate culture should include:
- Involvement in as many aspects of the business as possible so that the employee feels part of the team.
- Feedback and reinforcement so that employees know if they are performing their tasks to the standard required. If they are not, then feedback will help them improve their productivity. Reinforcement will give the worker a sense of pride because management has acknowledged their efforts.

Communications systems

Employers and employees can communicate with each other regarding the operation of the business. Good communication allows any disagreements or conflicts to be resolved. This communications system may involve:
- Grievance procedures which are designed to solve disputes in the workplace before they escalate into major events. In recent years the IRC has encouraged parties to use these procedures rather than proceeding to arbitration.
- Worker participation and team briefings provide an outlet for employees to have a say in the day-to-day running of the business. If employees sense ownership of projects or policy and are able to influence the way things are done, then there is often much less chance of conflict and therefore better employment relations. Team briefings allow management to inform employees about company policy and the reasons behind that policy.

Rewards

A business with a strong corporate culture will pay staff well in terms of financial and non-financial rewards.

Training and development

These programs are important if a firm is to maximise its productivity. Workers will tend to be more productive if they know their jobs and if they are familiar with the firms operating procedures.

Flexibility in the workplace

Flexible working hours include allowing staff to have time to pick up the children in the afternoons and attend school functions. Some businesses allow staff to work from home or work flexible shifts to suit their personal lifestyle. Others provide 'family and community leave' so that staff can attend to family matters or undertake essential community service. These conditions promote good personal relations between management and staff.

Benchmarking and key variables

This is another important way in which Human Resource Managers measure the effectiveness of the workforce. Benchmarking refers to the establishment points of reference from which quality or excellence is measured. Quality can come in two forms, the quality of the workforce itself and the quality of the work they produce.

The quality of the workforce is measured by their level of expertise which in turn is a reflection of their training. A well trained workforce will perform at a high level and be productive. In addition, many businesses strive to achieve 'world's best practice' in terms of their output. Therefore if the productivity of the workforce increases and high quality work is being produced in the firm then this is an indicator of effective human resource management.

Changes in staff turnover

This is another key indicator of the effectiveness of human resource management. When staff stay with an employer, the employer is likely to be highly regarded. The cost of finding new employees can be substantial, particularly executives. Stable employment usually indicates satisfaction with the organisation and their supervisors. Human resources managers are constantly trying to find ways to reduce staff turnover. This may be by:
- increased responsibility allowing for greater job satisfaction
- greater flexibility of working hours for domestic reasons
- clearer career paths so that promotion is a possibility for conscientious and well trained employees
- greater autonomy to make decisions without having to defer to a supervisor constantly
- generous sick leave entitlements especially for those who are suffering from work related illness

- better facilities such as a canteen, wash rooms and recreation room
- cleaner environment free from polluted air, water, and general rubbish
- increased pay will help reduce turnover by making the job attractive.

Absenteeism

The things that cause absenteeism include dissatisfaction with supervisors, the job or the lack of opportunity. No job will suit every employee, but the Human Resource Manager must try to make the job as satisfying as possible. This will reduce absenteeism and increase productivity in the workplace. Absenteeism is a huge cost to the business. Other workers have to cover for the absent employee or casual staff have to be employed to take their place for the period.

Accidents

This is a good indicator of human resource management effectiveness. The Human Resource Manager should ensure that all Occupational Health & Safety provisions are being adhered to and that training is taking place. A reduced accident rate will lead to a happier, more productive workplace.

Levels of disputation

A key factor in determining the effectiveness of human resource management is the level of disputation. Lower levels of industrial conflict are indicative of good relations between management and the workforce. It is also an indicator that effective human resource management practices are being implemented in the workplace.

Worker satisfaction

Worker satisfaction covers all of the areas discussed above. From benchmarking, staff turnover, absenteeism, accidents to levels of disputation, all these factors are indicators of satisfaction in the workplace.

REVISION EXERCISES 4.5

1. What is meant by the term 'corporate culture'?

   _____

   _____

   _____

2. Describe the **five** areas of corporate culture that are indicators of good human resource management.

   _____

   _____

   _____

   _____

   _____

3. What is meant by the term and 'benchmarking and key variables'?

   _____

   _____

   _____

   _____

   _____

   _____

4. Explain how changes in staff turnover, absenteeism, accidents, levels of disputation and worker satisfaction are indicators of good human resource management in a business.

   _____

   _____

   _____

   _____

   _____

   _____

   _____

   _____

PRACTICE SHORT ANSWER
STYLE QUESTIONS

1. Stakeholders in business can be defined as" anyone who has an interest in the business".
    Name **five** stakeholders in the Human Resources area and analyse their role in maintaining effective Human Resources.   (10 marks)

    1. _____

       _____

    2. _____

       _____

    3. _____

       _____

    4. _____

       _____

    5. _____

       _____

2. Four important influences on Human Resources are:
    a. Economic influences
    b. Technological influences
    c. Social influences
    d. Ethical influences

    Select two of those influences and analyse their role
    in the human resources process.   (10 marks)

    _____

    _____

    _____

    _____

    _____

    _____

    _____

    _____

3. The human resource process involves acquisition, development, maintenance and separation. Define each of the above processes and briefly describe how the efficient use of each can benefit a business.

(8 marks)

_____

_____

_____

_____

_____

_____

_____

_____

4. Define the following terms.

Job design and task description _____

_____

_____

_____

Training and development of new staff _____

_____

_____

_____

Performance management of new staff _____

_____

_____

_____

Rewards for performance _____

_____

_____

_____

_____

5. Select five indicators of good human resource management and describe and analyse the importance of each to a business   (10 marks)

    1. _____

    _____

    2. _____

    _____

    3. _____

    _____

    4. _____

    _____

    5. _____

    _____

6. Four important influences on Human Resources are:
    a. Economic influences
    b. Technological influences
    c. Social influences
    d. Ethical influences

    Select two of those influences and analyse their role in the human resources process   (10 marks)

    _____

    _____

    _____

    _____

    _____

    _____

    _____

    _____

    _____

    _____

    _____

    _____

    _____

    _____

    _____

    _____

Glossary

Australian Securities and Investment Commission (ASIC): A government body established to monitor and regulate Australia's corporations, markets and financial services.

Australian Securities Exchange (ASX): The Australian Securities Exchange (ASX) provides a forum for businesses and individuals to buy and sell shares.

Awards: An award is an enforceable document containing minimum terms and conditions of employment in addition to any legislated minimum terms.

Balance Sheet: This statement gives a summary of the financial position of a business at a particular point in time. It shows the assets and liabilities of the business together with the value of owners equity in the business.

Banks: Secure organisation which uses funds deposited for investment by customers to provide cash and loans as required. Banks also exchange currencies and and provide a venue for financial transactions. As a group, banks are by far the largest financial providers in Australia.

Benchmarking refers to the establishment points of reference from which quality or excellence is measured.

Bills of exchange: (see commercial bills)

Budgets: Budgets are quantitative forecasts that help guide the use of the financial inputs and outgoings of a business.

Capital expenditure budget: A schedule setting out the planned expenditure on new machinery, buldings, plant and equipment.

Cash flow budget: A schedule of expected receipts and expenditure for a business. It differs from a cash flow statement, because it relates to future cash flows.

Cash flow statement: A cash flow statement is a summary of the movements of cash during a given period of time.

Certified Agreement: A certified agreement is an agreement made between employers and employees regarding wages and conditions in a workplace which has been ratified and approved by an appropriate tribunal or commission.

Commercial bills: These are known as bills of exchange. They are a form of short term (business) loan where a borrower agrees to repay a cash advance in 30 ,60 or 90 days as agreed.

Communication skills: Skills which enable people to understand each other. If a manager communicates effectively his plans will be followed and the business will grow.

Competitive positioning: Is about defining how you'll "differentiate" your offering and create value for your market.

Competitive pricing: This occurs when prices are set in relation to competitors prices.

Computer aided design (CAD): Design functions are automated by using computers.

Computer aided manufacture (CAM): This is software which allows the manufacturing process to become controlled by a computer.

Consumer markets: These consist of all the individuals and households who buy goods and services for personal consumption.

Contract manufacturing: The practice of outsourcing production instead of producing the function in house.

Contract worker: A contract worker hires his labour on an hourly basis, instead of becoming an employee.

Control: This is one of the managerial functions like planning, organizing, staffing and directing. In quality management, it is the operative stage, and may be used to describe all of these functions.

Corporate responsibility: The responsibility that business has to other businesses and the community generally.

Cost centre: A cost centre is a location, function or items of equipment monitored to determine operating costs for control purposes.

Cost control: Cost control involves careful purchasing, minimizing waste and efficient inventory control.

Cost leadership: This is an operating policy producing goods or services at the lowest cost possible to the business. Lower costs maximises profits, enabling business to establish a competitive advantage over its competitors.

Cost pricing: Selling goods at the producer's historical cost, i.e without making a profit.

Credit terms: These are the conditions of sale setting out how goods will be paid for, and the time to pay (30, 60 or 90 days).

Current assets: Consist of assets that can be turned into cash in a short period of time (usually within the accounting period). Current assets include cash, accounts receivable, inventories (which can be turned to cash quickly) and cash paid in advance.

Current liabilities: These are liabilities that may be called on in the short term (within one accounting period) and include accounts payable and overdrafts.

Customer orientation: When identifying consumer needs the marketer must identify what the consumer wants.

Customisation: Is the personalisation of products and services for individual customers.

Customise: To customise is to modify something according to a customer's individual requirements.

Data Miners: These are organisations which use huge data bases to pin point consumer preferences.

Debentures: A debenture is a loan to a company that is not necessarily secured by a mortgage on specific property but secured by the overall assets of the company.

Deceptive and misleading advertising: This occurs when, in the promotion of a product or service, a representation is made to the public that is false or misleading.

Demographics: Age, income, gender, marital status, sex, income etc

Derivatives: These are simple financial contracts whose value is linked to or derived from an underlying asset, such as stocks, bonds, commodities, loans and exchange rates.

De-skilling: This occurs when changed procedures (usually as a result of technology) removes a job that once required skill and replaces it with a job that doesn't.

Discounts: These are given on goods and services to encourage consumers to buy the product.

Discounts for early payments: Many businesses offer discounts to debtors for early payments as a means of improving cash flow.

Distribution channels: This covers the way in which a product is distributed from the factory to the consumer.

Double Loop learning: results in radical changes in the way the company does business. Double-loop learning allows the organisation to break out of existing thought patterns and to create a new mindset.

Effective profitability management: Refers to the maximisation of revenue and the minimisation of costs.

Efficiency: Describes how well a business is being run i.e. how efficiently the business is using its resources such as labour, finance or equipment.

e-marketing or electronic marketing: refers to the application of marketing principles and techniques via electronic media and more specifically the Internet.

Employees: People who work for employers for a wage or salary.

Employer associations: advise employers of their rights and obligations with regard to their employees and provide representation at Industrial Relations Commission (IRC) hearings where necessary.

Employers or management: is the group of people who own and manage a business.

Employment Contract: An employment contract is an agreement between an employer and employee/s that defines the rights and conditions for work.

Enterprise Agreement: An enterprise agreement is an agreement between an employer and an employee or employee group which covers wages and terms and conditions of work.

Equal Employment Opportunity (EEO): An employment policy where employees and employers have the responsibility to work to their full capacity, to recognise the skills and talents of other staff members to respect cultural and social diversity among colleagues and customers, to refuse to co-operate in, or condone any behaviour that may harass a colleague. (www.lawlink.nsw.gov.au)

Equity: Refers to the capital and accumulated funds and reserves shown in the balance sheet that is the owners share of a business.

Equity finance: The money (capital) put into a business by its owners. This may consist of cash, shares purchased in the business or retained profits. (See retained profits)

Exchange rate: i.e. the value of one currency against another.

Expense budgets: A forecast of all the activities of a business and the associated expenses involved.

Expense minimisation: A policy or practice of producing goods or services at the lowest possible cost or expenditure.

External funds: are the funds used in a business that have been obtained from a source outside the business. This is usually in the form of debt finance.

Factoring: This is the selling of accounts receivable to a financier. This is regarded as an important source of finance because the business is receiving immediate funds to use as working capital.

FIFO (First -In-First Out): An asset-management and valuation method in which the assets produced or acquired first are sold, used or disposed of first. FIFO may be used by a individual or a corporation.

Fixed cost: A fixed cost is a cost to a business that has to be made regardless of the level of output.

Flat Management Structures: As a response to change, flatter management structures have become more common over the past ten years. Businesses adopt a flatter management structure to reduce the number of levels of management, giving greater responsibility to middle managers.

Flexible employees: work flexible hours according to need. The conditions here are similar to casual employees unless a permanent employment agreement is decided on.

Flexible work practices: These are patterns of work that allow employees to vary their work commitments around the pressures of other responsibilities. They can assist employees in effectively managing work and family duties.

Foreign exchange (forex) market: The forex market is where currencies are traded by financial institutions acting as buyers and sellers.

Gantt chart: is a sequencing tool presented as a bar graph with time and activities shown on the two axes.

Global branding: This refers to the use of a brand name that is known world-wide.

Globalisation: Globalisation is the bringing together all of the world's economies for the purposes of trade and culture. It is the removing of barriers--trade barriers, language barriers, cultural barriers. It leads to the freeing up of the movement of labour from one country to another, the unification of laws and the unification of currency. It also involves financial flows, investment, technology and general economic behaviour in and between nations.

Global pricing: This is a contract between a customer and a supplier where the supplier agrees to charge the customer the same price for the delivery of parts or services anywhere in the world.

Global sourcing: This refers to the action of a business sourcing its raw materials from anywhere in the world. It is also a term used to describe the practice of sourcing raw materials from the global market for goods and services across geopolitical boundaries.

Goodwill: Goodwill is an intangible asset equal to that part of total assets which cannot be attributed to the separate business assets. In some ways it represents the synergy of the business.

Greenfields agreements: These involve a genuinely new enterprise that one or more employers are establishing or propose to establish and who have not yet employed persons necessary for the normal conduct of the enterprise. Such agreements may be either a single-enterprise agreement or a multi-enterprise agreement.

Growth: Business growth occurs with increased sales, by merging with other businesses or acquiring other businesses. In the balance sheet, growth is measured by the growth in the value of the business assets.

Head hunting: Recruitment by directly targeting a key individual who has the qualifications and characteristics that the firm is seeking. The prospect may already hold down a job in another business. The 'head hunter' usually makes an offer which, if accepted, enables the appointment to be made.

Historic cost: is the practice of valuing assets at the time of purchase.

Human Resource Management: This involves the use of qualified management staff in achieving the goals of the business, by ensuring that staff are productive, well-trained and satisfied in their jobs.

Implied conditions:

Consumers can expect the following when goods are sold:
1. the vendor is entitled to sell
2. the goods are unencumbered
3. the consumer has the right to quiet enjoyment
4. goods will comply with their description
5. goods will be of merchantable quality and fit for the purpose
6. goods will comply with a sample
7. services will be rendered with due care and skill
8. goods supplied with the service will be fit for purpose
9. services will be fit for the purpose.

Income statement: (see revenue/profit & loss statement)

Induction: This is the systematic introduction of new employees to their jobs, co-workers and the organisation. It may include on the job training.

Industrial markets: These are markets for goods and services which are used in the production of other goods and services and which are on sold to others in the production process.

Innovation: Innovation refers to the introduction of new systems, new technologies, approaches and products.

Inputs: These are the resources used in the process of production.

Intangibles: These are things such as patents, copyrights, trademarks and brand names and are often difficult to quantify.

Interest rates: are the price expressed as a percentage per annum for borrowing or lending money.

Intermediate goods: Those goods manufuctered from raw materials and then used to make a finished product.

Intermediate markets: Often known as reseller markets. These markets consist of businesses that acquire goods for the purpose of reselling them to others in order to make a profit.

Internal sources of finance: are those funds provided to the business by its owners and are in the form of retained profits.

Interpersonal skills: Effective managers are be able to interact with their staff to enable the business to run smoothly. Skilful communication ensures tasks are perfomed efficiently and productively

Inventories: Inventories are raw materials, goods in transit and complete and incomplete work (work in progress). Inventories are expensive and can often comprise 50% of working capital

Job design: Job design determines the way work is organised and performed. The process identifies the work to be done, how the job will be done, the skills, knowledge and abilities (capabilities) needed to do the job and how the job contributes to achieving organisational goals.

Kaizen: This is the Japanese concept of constantly seeking improvement and questioning current methods of production.

Leadership style: The manner and approach of providing direction, implementing plans, and motivating people.

Leasing: This is an agreement whereby the owner of an asset (lessor) allows the use of an asset by a lessee for a periodic charge.

LIFO (last-in-first-out): An asset-management and valuation method that assumes that assets produced or acquired last are the ones that are used, sold or disposed of first.

Line management: Management of a business concerned with acquiring, producing and supplying goods and services to consumers. (Other management is involved in supporting line managers pursue these objectives. Human resource and administration managers would fall into this support function.)

Liquidity: is the ability of a business to pay its short term obligations as they fall due.

List pricing: This is the price a product is set at on a sellers' schedule. The list price is the normal selling price without discounts.

Logistics: Logistics is the internal and external transport, storage and distribution resources of a business

Long-term borrowing: These are regarded as borrowings that will take longer than a year to repay.

Loss leader: A loss leader is a product sold at a low price (at cost or below cost) to stimulate other profitable sales.

Maintenance of human resources: This is the "keeping" of human resources by providing them with benefits such as a safe working environment, good pay and a fair and equitable industrial setting in which to work.

Management: Management is the process of integrating all the available resources of the business to achieve the aims of the organisation.

Management Consultant: A management consultant is someone from outside the business who, for a fee will come in to advise the business about problems with systems and procedures that the business cannot solve on its own.

Management control system: This is a system which gathers and uses information to evaluate the performance of different parts of the business or resources

Marketing: The coordination of activities that determine the product, price promotion and place (the Four P's) for a product or service.

Marketing aim: To meet the objectives of a business by satisfying a customer's needs and wants

Market penetration: This is strength of sales and marketing of the business and its product compared to the total market size.

Market pricing: This occurs where a business prices their product according to what the business feels the market can pay.

Marketing concept: The marketing plan or strategy adopted by a business seeking to satisfy consumer demand.

Market research: Is the systematic collection and analysis of information and findings relating to a marketing situation faced by a company.

Market Share: Expressed as a percentage of the available market for the product. For example if the total market is 100%, the share held by company X might be 6.5%

Market share analysis: This analysis involves comparing the market share of the business with ones competition.

Mentoring: This is a situation where a more experienced (usually older) staff member is assigned to look after the progress of a new employee in the workplace.

Middle Management: The level of management between top management and other workers. There may be a number of levels in a large business. Middle levels are progressively being reduced as business seeks greater efficiency and empathy with its staff.

Minimum employment standards: These relate to the minimum conditions under which an employee can be employed.

Mortgage: This is a loan giving a bank first claim over specified assets such as land or buildings which are used as security.

Motivation: This refers to the energy, direction, purpose and effort displayed by people in their activities.

Multi-enterprise agreements: These involve two or more employers that are not all single interest employers. competitors.

New issues (shares): This occurs when a private or public company wishes to raise more capital and issues a new issue of shares.

Niche markets: are small, specialised markets catering for a small clientele.

Nominal exchange rate risks: This refers to the risk of losing money on international transactions as a result of changes in the exchange rate i.e. a depreciation of the Australian dollar or an appreciation of the currency of the country we are dealing with thus forcing us to take a loss on the transaction.

Non-current assets: These are those assets that are held for a long period of time (longer than the accounting period). Assets that cannot easily be converted into cash.

Non-current liabilities: These are held for a long period of time (usually several years) and include mortgages and long-term borrowings.

Observation: This is the gathering of data through the observation of people, activity or results.

Operations/management: Operations or operations management can be described as the allocation and maintenance of machinery and resources (for example raw materials and labour), productivity, quality, wastage and the introduction of new technologies that will combine to produce a good or service. Operations may also refer to a wider sphere of production such as assembly, batching, creative design and packaging. It is sometimes also referred to as production management.

Outsourcing: This is a situation whereby a business contracts certain work "out" to professionals such as lawyers and accountants.

Operational planning: Making decisions about which groups or departments will be responsible for carrying out the various elements of the strategic plan, deciding what needs to be done, when, by whom and at what cost.

Opinion leaders: are used to promote a product by promoting it in written form or verbally.

Ordinary shares: These are shares issued to investors in companies that entitle purchasers (holders) to a part ownership of the business.

Outsourcing: This is a situation whereby a business contracts certain work "out" to professionals such as lawyers and accountants.

Overdrafts: An overdraft is an agreement between a bank and a business allowing the business to overdraw on its cheque account up to a certain, agreed figure.

Owners equity: This consists of funds placed into the business by its owners. They can also be described as the assets that the business holds on behalf of the owners and includes shares and retained profits.

Part-time employees: Can be permanent except they work reduced hours. For example a part-time teacher may work two or three days a week.

Payment period: These periods vary according to the amount borrowed and for what purpose. Borrowings may be free of interest for short periods or attract interest for longer periods.

Penetration pricing: This involves charging a very low price initially to generate high volume sales and gain market share. It is used to establish customers that will be loyal to the product in the long term.

People Skills: Those skills associated with the management of employees through leadership, good communication and interest in employees ambitions and progress.

Performance management: or appraisal is the process of assessing the performance of employees against actual results and expectations of the manager.

Permanent employees: Employees who hold down a job with security of tenure. They receive benefits such as compulsory superannuation, holiday pay and sick leave.

Physical evidence: Is the material part of a service. In marketing it may be the tickets, brochures or advertising: the non-physical part may be the entertainment of the spectacle provided by the sport.

Place: The methods of distribution, storage and delivery that are used for the product.

Political and default risk: This risk is associated with countries which have unstable governments or those that have a difficult balance of payments situation.

Potential market: is the set of consumers who have some level of interest in a product.

Price: The cost of the product in the market place together with the methods of pricing used, discounts or credit terms used.

Price discrimination: This occurs when a seller charges different prices to different consumers for the same product.

Price points: These are points where the price of a product is at its optimum i.e. at the point where a retailer will sell most of their products for maximum profit.

Price skimming: This can be applied to a new product that is attractive and which has little or no competition. A high price can be charged initially, but can only be maintained over the short term because the high price will attract competitors into the market and the new competition will force the price downwards.

Primary research: This involves collecting raw data from scratch i.e. data that has not been published elsewhere.

Process layouts: These are configurations in which operations of a similar nature or function are grouped together.

Product: All the different goods and services that are offered to customers, the way they are packaged and the types of after sales service offered.

Product approach: The product approach revolves around the idea that if producers produced products and services, then consumers would want them.

Product differentiation: can be defined as the variation between a number of models of the same basic product e.g. a brand of washing machine with six available models.

Product positioning: This is a key aspect of the marketing mix. It's the image a product has in the mind of a consumer. Products can be positioned in the market according to price and quality, image, target market or its competition.

Profitability: This refers to the yield or profit a business receives in return for its productive effort.

Proliferation: When a product category contains many brands with minor differences.

Promotion: This is the technique of presenting a product or service to a customer in such a way that the customer will want to purchase that product or service.

Promotional pricing: This involves a temporary reduction in price on a number of products on offer designed to increase sales in the short term and give the retail outlet a boost.

Public relations: This is any form of letting the customer know that a product exists and can involve any of the promotional methods. Publicity may involve such things as testimonial letters, word of mouth information, spotters fees and sponsorships of special events and sporting teams.

Quality assurance: The QA manager's role is to count, measure and report on all aspects of operations to enable the line manager to direct and supervise. QA reports will highlight any deviation from planned or standard performance and suggest what corrective action needs to be taken.

Quality Circles: These comprise groups of skilled employees gathered together in a process that aims to better the quality of a product/service or procedure that will benefit a customer or the business by decreasing unnecessary costs.

Quality control: This can be defined as the management procedures that are put in place to check the suitability of raw materials, progress of production and product output to minimise reprocessing, seconds, wastage, costs, warranty claims and service problems.

Quality Expectations: see **Quality Assurance**

Quality management: This involves control, assurance and improvement. It is a continuously cyclical process calling on all the entrepreneurial flair, innovative skills, experience, people management skills, decision making skills, communication skills that a manager has.

Recruitment: This involves the ways in which employees are acquired for the firm.

Redundancy payments: When a worker is no longer needed in the business, he becomes redundant, and receives compensation for losing his job.

Relationship marketing: A marketing strategy relying on a personal relationship with customers.

Research and Development: refers to "creative work undertaken on a systematic basis in order to increase the stock of knowledge, including knowledge of man, culture and society, and the use of this stock of knowledge to devise new applications" (OECD).

Resignation: The voluntary action taken by an employee to leave an employer.

Resistance to change: The unwillingness of employees or managers to embrace new practices. The source of change may be new technology, new inventions, new ideas or new stakeholders.

Resource markets: Are those markets for commodities such as minerals, agricultural products, people looking for work (human resources) and financial resources.

Retained profits: These are the profits retained by the business and which have not been distributed to the owners/shareholders in the form of dividends.

Return on capital: This is the percentage of profit before or after tax compared to the value of capital (money) invested in the business.

Revenue controls: These are aimed at maximising revenues received by the business through its business and financial activities.

Revenue/Profit & Loss Statement: This statement provides a summary of the trading operations of a business for a given period of time (usually one month or a year).

Robotics: The use of robots or automation to streamline operations, often eliminating boring repetitive tasks.

Sale and lease back: A device used by business to sell assets and lease them back from the purchaser. This then frees up capital that can be used for other purposes.

Sales mix: This refers to the mix of the products produced and offered for sale by a business.

Sales objectives: These relate to the concept of increasing and maximising sales in order to maximise revenue.

Scanning and Learning: is a process of gathering, analysing, and dispensing business information for tactical (short term) or strategic (long term) purposes.

Scheduling: This involves the time taken to complete a particular job.

Secondary research: Data that is already in existence and usually collected by someone else for some other purpose.

Seconds: These are goods which have failed to meet the design or quality standards of the business.

Security: The charge given over an asset or assets which will be given over to a lender if the borrower defaults on a loan.

Short-term borrowing: This is made up of overdrafts and commercial bills and is normally used when the business requires finance for a relatively short time of up to a year or when the finance is required to assist with working capital.

Separation of human resources: This is the business term that describes the reduction of staff numbers for a variety of reasons, including retirement and redundancy (including voluntary and involuntary redundancy).

Sequencing: This involves placing tasks into an order so that an operation runs smoothly.

Sales promotion: Sales promotions may take several different forms. A trade fair such as a motor show, computer show, sports or leisure show is one form of sales promotion. The producer demonstrates his/her wares in an area set aside for that particular business while potential customers can walk by and observe the products on show.

Secondary Industry: The industrial sector of an economy dominated by the manufacture of finished products.

Secondary target market: This is the second most important market identified as a consumer group for the output of the business.

Self-managing: Employees in a self managed business work in an autonomous fashion without the need for constant supervision.

Situation analysis: A situation analysis is an assessment of a business's current position, e.g. its market share, profitability or competition

Stakeholders: Stakeholders are those people or institutions with an interest in a business in some way.

Strategic alliance: A strategic alliance occurs where two or more businesses work together to achieve a particular goal.

Strategic analysis: Strategic analysis is the examination of a business in the light of long term (3 to 5 years) goals and objectives. It will usually consider budgets, forecasts and prospects

Strategic planning: Strategic planning is long term planning (3 to 5 years).

Strategic thinking: This is the ability to think beyond the immediate tasks.

Target market: This is a section of the public to whom the producer aims his/her products and marketing campaigns.

Teamwork: The ability to work together. If the manager is a "team player" he will inspire teamwork in employees.

Training: This is the preparation of employees to undertake existing or new tasks proficiently.

Variable costs: Those costs only incurred when something is produced, such as direct labour or raw materials used. They vary directly with the volume of sales or production.

Vision: This is the ability of management to see where the business needs to go in the future and what is required to succeed. It is also the ability to see the "big picture" with regard to business direction.

Voluntary administration: This is a process under the Corporations Act. It allows a caretaker (the voluntary administrator) to take control of the affairs of a company while the directors are given a chance to propose a resolution of the company's financial problems to its creditors.

Voluntary separation and Involuntary separation: Voluntary separation occurs when an employee leaves of their own free will. Involuntary separation occurs when an employee loses their job as a result of an employer's action.